ROBERT D. SMITH

20,000 DAYS

...and Counting

The Crash Course for Mastering Your Life Right Now

simple truths®
Your Destination For Inspiration
an imprint of Sourcebooks, Inc.

Editing by: Alice Patenaude

Photo Credits:
Cover: front, Christopher Meder/Thinkstock; back, MaxyM/Shutterstock
Internals: page 1, Christopher Meder/Thinkstock; pages 2–3, LilKar/Shutterstock; page 4, studioworxx/Thinkstock; page 5, MaxyM/Shutterstock; pages 14–15, Purestock/Thinkstock; pages 16–17, Andrew_Mayovskyy/Thinkstock; page 21, Sarunyu_foto/Shutterstock; page 23, Givaga/Thinkstock; pages 24–25, digidreamgrafix/Thinkstock; page 31, amnachphoto/Shutterstock; pages 38–39, pigphoto/Thinkstock; pages 44–45, Givaga/Thinkstock; page 55, Janoka82/Thinkstock; pages 56–57, TomasSereda/Thinkstock; page 63, Andrew_Mayovskyy/Thinkstock; pages 64–65, kojihirano/Thinkstock; pages 68–69, ArtamaPhotography/Thinkstock; pages 72–73, Simotion/Thinkstock; pages 74–75, MariuszBlach/Thinkstock; pages 78–79, MariuszBlach/Thinkstock; pages 84–85, FotoYakov/Shutterstock; pages 90–91, cgardinerphotos/Thinkstock; pages 94–95, Galyna Andrushko/Shutterstock; pages 98–99, Angelo Ferraris/Shutterstock; pages 104–105, Nikiforov Alexander/Shutterstock; page 109, fakruljamil/Thinkstock; pages 110–111, ventdusud/Thinkstock; pages 112–113, MartinM303/Thinkstock; page 117, Brand X Pictures/Thinkstock; pages 118–119, Purestock/Thinkstock; pages 122–123, dkolsek/Thinkstock; page 127, Andrew_Mayovskyy/Thinkstock; pages 128–129, Biletskiy_Evgeniy/Thinkstock; page 133, TomasSereda/Thinkstock; pages 134–135, Design Pics/Thinkstock; pages 136–137, FWPhotographer/Thinkstock; pages 138–139, Elenathewise/Thinkstock.

Published by Simple Truths, an imprint of Sourcebooks, Inc.
P.O. Box 4410, Naperville, Illinois 60567-4410
(630) 961-3900
Fax: (630) 961-2168
www.sourcebooks.com

Originally published in 2012 in the United States by Thomas Nelson Publishers.

Printed and bound in China.
OGP 10 9 8 7 6 5 4 3 2 1

The last four decades have been influenced by a friend, confidant, business partner, guide, and influencer—a true "noticer." He's someone I have talked to almost every day since I met him when he was in ninth grade. Our friendship amazes even us. I am honored and blessed to call him a gift from God: Andy Andrews.

Contents

Foreword
by Andy Andrews

I met him for the first time when I was fourteen years old. It was the summer before I entered the ninth grade and, along with a bunch of other guys from our area, I headed to church camp for a week. My cabin counselor was a freshman in college. His name was Robert D. Smith. And he's been counseling me ever since!

Actually, it wasn't until I was out of college that we formalized an arrangement. I was to be "the talent." He would be "the manager." Frankly, I talked him into it. You see, Robert was aware that he knew nothing about entertainment or publishing or recording. But I knew Robert possessed qualities that were more powerful than mere knowledge about any particular subject could ever be.

First, he had a deep desire to follow God's direction.

Second, Robert had become a master of self-discipline.

Third, he had a boundless enthusiasm that was contagious to everyone with whom he came in contact.

Fourth, he had a genuine hunger to produce the very best of everything he touched.

Fifth, people liked him. A lot.

To this day, Robert is the best I have ever seen at creating instant, lifelong friends. Do you know how much of a business advantage that is?

What if almost everybody you met for years was interested in helping you? What if, every day, there were people around the world thinking toward and praying for your success?

The most remarkable thing to me about Robert is not the huge agencies in New York and Los Angeles whose clients he has turned down for years. It's not the unblemished track record he has recorded with the first client he accepted (me). The most remarkable thing about Robert is that, almost without exception, for more than three decades, every huge win he has orchestrated in businesses across the board was a rejection or failure *first*.

The most remarkable thing about Robert for YOU, however, is a completely different thing. This unbelievable treasure I am about to serve you on a silver platter should stun, amaze, and excite you.

Are you ready?

Here it is…

The most remarkable thing for you about Robert D. Smith's life, his success, is that it is transparent, duplicable, and outlined in this book. I can promise that what you are about to read will change you.

If you will allow the change!

You see, Robert's incredible consistency in achieving so much throughout the years has very little to do with what he has done. His success has everything to do with what he has become and the person he continues to be in the process of becoming. Robert's success, at a base level, has come because of the way he thinks. The way he has trained himself to think has become his behavior—the way he acts. His actions have created his reputation, and, of course, his reputation is first-class and worldwide.

Everything you need to know to create a basis for where you want to be is here in this book. These are the very thoughts, directions, and techniques Robert D. Smith has used to guide every aspect of my career for thirty-five years.

So read quickly. Read carefully. And read with a highlighter! This is *highly* valuable information.

Andy Andrews

New York Times bestselling author of *How Do You Kill*
11 Million People?, The Noticer, and *The Traveler's Gift*

Orange Beach, Alabama

Author's Note

I wrote this book so you could read it quickly.

Why?

Because today could be your last day.

Because life is too short.

Because you need to understand what you are about to read immediately.

Because asking for more than an hour of your time is truly asking a lot.

You have important things to do. Critical tasks to accomplish. Milestones to celebrate. More lives to touch.

So read with purpose. Read with a sense of urgency. Read with anticipation.

This is not a book to be used for passing the time; it's a

book to be used for squeezing every last day, hour, minute, and second out of life until your life is done and you've given, loved, and celebrated all you could.

A hundred years from now, no one who is reading this will be alive. The world will be filled with new generations.

A hundred years from now, what will you have left behind? What will your legacy be?

Are you ready to find out?

Let's begin.

Section 1

The 20,000-Day Mind-Set

Robert D. Smith

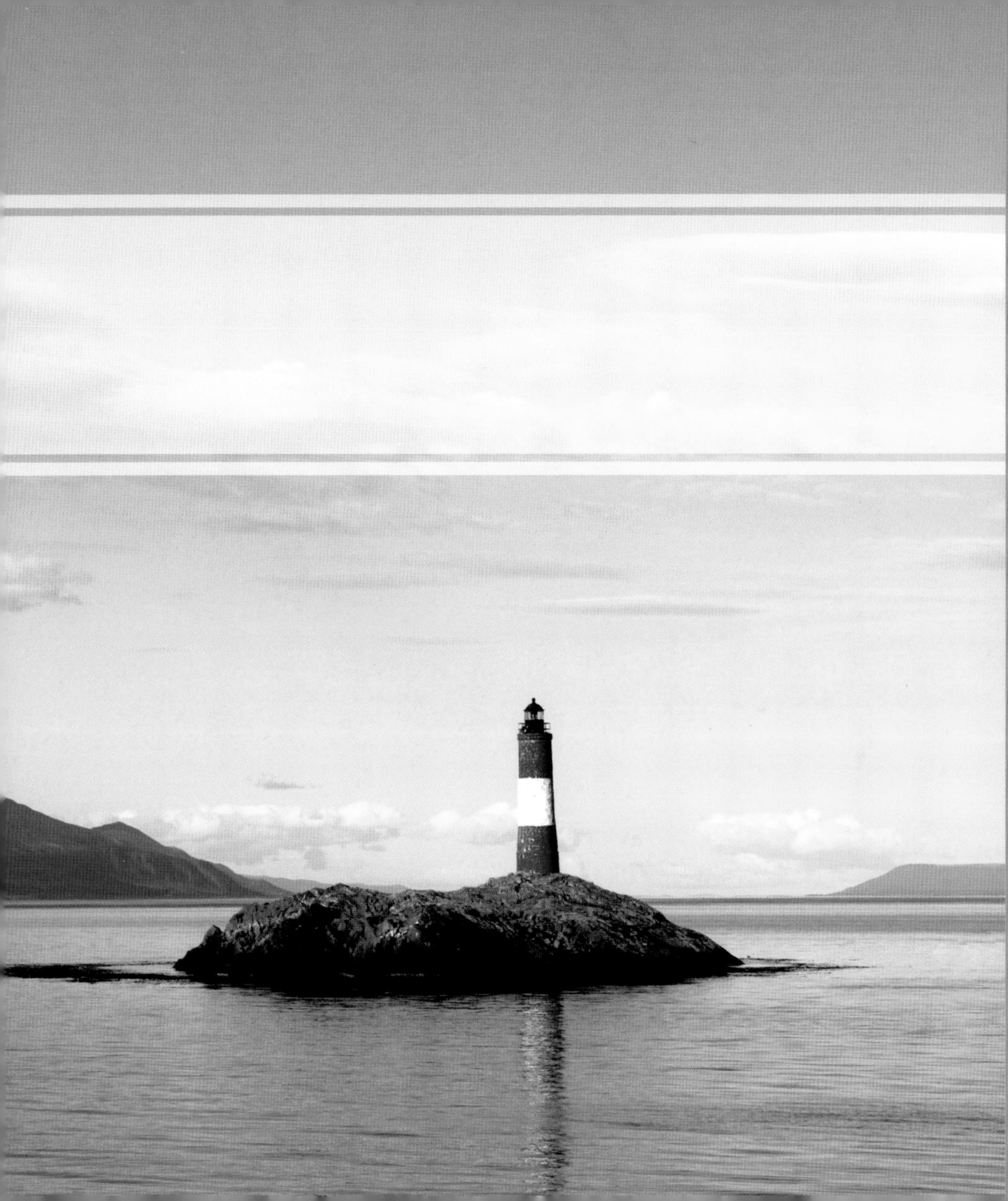

20,000 Days...and Counting

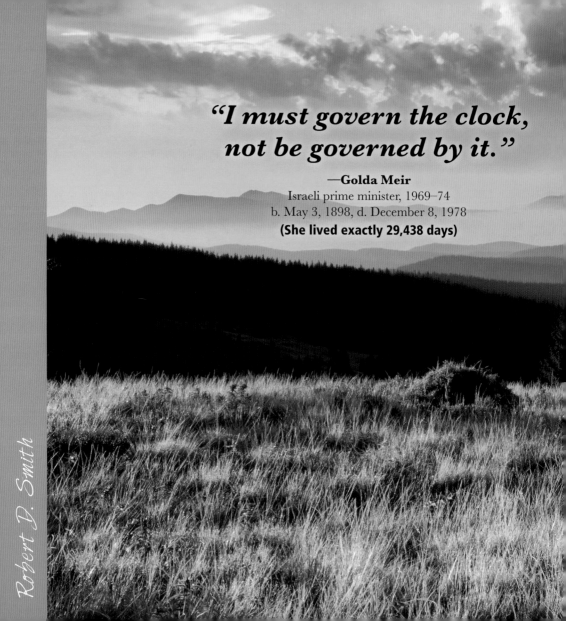

"*I must govern the clock,
not be governed by it.*"

—**Golda Meir**
Israeli prime minister, 1969–74
b. May 3, 1898, d. December 8, 1978
(She lived exactly 29,438 days)

Robert P. Smith

20,000 Days...and Counting

20,000 Days...and Counting

In 2009, midway through my fifty-fourth year living on this planet, I came to a realization that changed my life forever: I had been alive for nearly 20,000 days!

That's 480,000 hours.

28,800,000 minutes.

1,728,000,000 seconds.

Yet even with all those days, all those hours, all those minutes and seconds that had already passed, I had this overwhelming feeling that I still had so much more to do. I am aware of the fragility of life, yet somehow I continue to be shocked at how rapidly the days fly by. To this point, my life has slipped past so quickly I can hardly comprehend it.

I am blessed beyond belief with parents who have loved and encouraged me, and are proud of who I am still in the process of

Robert P. Smith

becoming. I have three sisters, all of whom have incredible families. I look forward to every moment with them.

I knew what I wanted to study years before I went to college. I attended Samford University in Birmingham, Alabama, majoring in psychology, minoring in speech and drama, and acquiring a secondary teaching certificate.

During the three years after graduation, I held a variety of jobs. Those included being a youth director for a church, selling cars, and acting as sales manager for a company that produced surgical stainless steel. At the age of twenty-five, I was asked to go into artist management. My only client was to be a friend I had met seven years earlier when he was in the ninth grade. That friend's name was Andy Andrews.

For the last three decades, I have been privileged to manage this one act. He started as a comedian on cruise ships, then headlined the college circuit for years before performing in arenas and major showrooms in Las Vegas with Kenny Rogers, Joan Rivers, Randy Travis, Cher, and many others.

Eventually, Andy transitioned from comedian to author of what most would call "inspirational" books. We self-published a series of books called *Storms of Perfection* that sold over 600,000 copies…before Amazon existed. As far as publishing is concerned, Andy's tipping point happened when Thomas Nelson Publishers published his first novel, *The Traveler's Gift*. More about that later.

Bottom line: I am a behind-the-scenes guy. I have never had any desire to be onstage or even write a book. So yes, I am just as surprised as anyone that you are reading this. In fact, what you are about to read has always been for my eyes only. These are my personal notes about life and business, from journals that no one has ever seen.

But enough about the past; let's talk about *the future*.

What can you and I do right now in order to make the most out of the years in front of us? What can we do to accomplish more, to celebrate more, to touch more lives in our remaining years than we have to this point?

How can we live our next days to the fullest?

I am definitely one to plan things out. Planning is natural for me to do; *however*, on my 20,000th day, I did something entirely out of character. I packed a few things, hopped in the car, and drove.

When the time seemed right, I stopped and checked into one of the leading hotels of the world with a single objective in mind for the next forty-eight hours: to celebrate my first 20,000 days by putting myself through a crash course in planning my *next* 20,000 days.

Consider this book your personal crash course. Following are the specific breakthroughs I took away from my 20,000-day planning period. Here are the thoughts and actions I have pledged to implement daily for the rest of my life so that I live with intense purpose, constant joy, and lasting influence.

Robert D. Smith

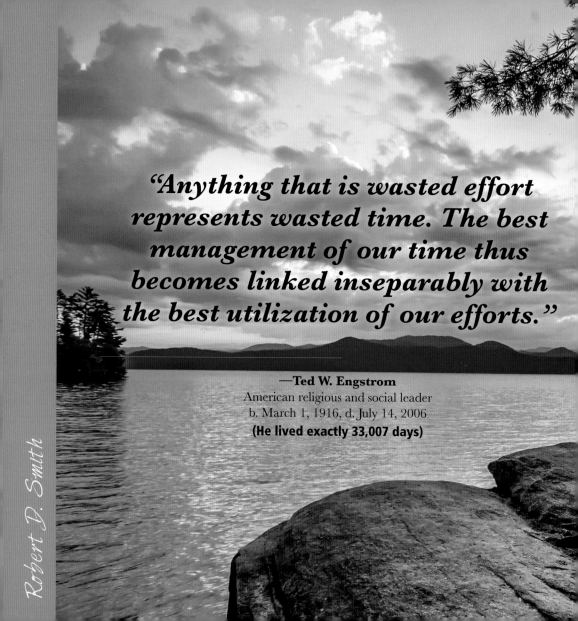

"*Anything that is wasted effort represents wasted time. The best management of our time thus becomes linked inseparably with the best utilization of our efforts.*"

—**Ted W. Engstrom**
American religious and social leader
b. March 1, 1916, d. July 14, 2006
(He lived exactly 33,007 days)

Robert D. Smith

20,000 Days...and Counting

5/5/55

My birth date, May 5, 1955, causes some people to speculate that the date must mean something. If so, I don't know what. Some think all those fives are auspicious and should be considered my lucky number. Others have suggested that I play it in the lottery. But I don't gamble.

I was honored and privileged when Andy Andrews and his wife, Polly, threw me a surprise fiftieth birthday party. How nearly ninety people could possibly show up at one location without me ever having a hint of what was going on from any family, friends, or associates is still beyond me. If you've ever experienced a truly happy surprise, then you can understand what I mean. It was simply amazing—a memory created for eternity!

Out of gratitude, I called Andy late that night because I wanted to share something I had never told anyone.

In my ninth-grade PE class, a good friend of mine, Paul Kartlick, tripped while playing basketball, hit his head hard on the outdoor concrete court, and died. Gone at fourteen years old. I was stunned. Shocked to my core.

I had been raised in the church and was very aware of God and spiritual things, but this hit me hard. It was my first realization that I am always, very literally, only one step away from dying. Any moment. Any day. Anywhere.

If you've ever experienced a tragedy, you probably have a good idea of how I was feeling. It was a pivotal point—a transition of some kind. Almost immediately, I began to reassess everything I thought I knew about life. We've all heard that life can change in an instant, but when that change results in the loss of life itself, it can become a huge and incredibly defining moment.

Since that day, I have lived with the odd sense that I, too, might die young. This experience and the feeling it fostered in me created a unique sense of urgency. Even at a young age I began to seek out ways to fulfill my purpose. There had to be a purpose to life, right? Every day became a major mission to find out why I was here and what I was supposed to do with my life.

I may not have fully realized my life's purpose as a freshman in high school, but I reasoned that it had to be a ton of little things adding up to something big. I had no idea what "big" looked like, but I understood little things. Consequently, I felt a pressing desire to accomplish these little things—make a phone call, write a letter, research an idea—as soon as they occurred to me. I constantly asked myself, *What is important now? What is next?* I could never escape those two questions as they spun around in my mind.

To this day, those same two questions keep me up late, get me up early, and create a never-ending quest of enormous possibilities and accomplishments. In truth, I never really want to be finished, though I am aware that one day, it will all end. But not yet.

I know I will die, but I do not know how long I will live.

To some, the very idea stated above may seem like a burden, but to me it's been a tremendous gift. Actually, it has been my motivating force.

With this thought weighing heavily on my mind, and added to the somewhat shocking revelation that I had been alive for 20,000 days, the first thing I did upon arriving at the hotel was to write and send forty-eight individual emails to the closest people in my life.

Every single one of them responded, many with an intense reaction. Some called. Some still talk about this email to this day.

The following concept, if applied—will change your life immediately and forever.

From: **Robert D. Smith**

Subject: 20,000 Days & Counting

Date: February 6, 2010 6:11:50 PM CST

To: (48 undisclosed individual recipients)

A couple of years ago, I found a widget called a countdown calendar that told me how many more days were left until New Year's Day, or whatever future date you put. I wondered if it worked on days past. It did. I put in my birth date and was WOWED by how many days I had been alive.

I decided then that I would do something to celebrate when I reached the next big number.

Friday, February 5, 2010, was that day. I had been alive 20,000 days as of that day. I am grateful for each day, and for where they have brought me.

I decided to celebrate by taking a forty-eight-hour crash course on planning the next 20,000 days, all while staying in a beautiful suite at one of the leading hotels of the world—at an undisclosed location.

LIFE IS SHORT.

OUR DAYS ARE NUMBERED.

OUR LIVES ARE LIMITED.

LIFE CAN PASS EXTREMELY FAST.

Five Benefits of Remembering That My Life Is Short

1. I will gain critical wisdom.

Counting my days has created a sense of intense urgency, causing me to choose how I am going to live and know what I am living for now.

I must desire wisdom with all my might. Wisdom is not only critical, but also valuable for me to make important daily decisions.

Robert D. Smith

2. I will be pushed to maximize my relationships.

It is so easy to take my relationships for granted. Counting my days reminds me of how precious they are. This causes me to be more loving, more forgiving, and more unselfish. Time is merely the measure of passing events. Time is inflexible. You cannot manage it. It cannot be compressed or expanded. Bottom line: don't focus on time, but on events themselves. When you control the event, you control your life. Fill these events with people you love. Relationships will be enhanced and memories created.

3. I will dedicate 100 percent of my life to God daily.

Counting my days compels me to want to spend my remaining days and years serving my Creator. I must stay watchful, alert, and committed.

I am grateful for every moment. Every possibility. Every person I meet throughout the day. I am fully open to God. I am an empty vessel to fill, a building with no doors. I seek what to do and where to go, living on the edge of great expectations.

The sum of what I do today is more expansive and far-reaching than I can comprehend. This gives me certainty to continue with tons of massive action all day.

4. I will possess a crystal clear vision for my life.

A vision or dream has given me direction, something to aim at, to work toward. It keeps me marching forward.

I do not want to close my eyes and fail to see the vision. I face today with my eyes wide open, actively looking for the next action to take. Today I will practice love in all my actions, taking calculated risks and living more adventurously.

I know I am creating a life book. Today is but a chapter—maybe even just a few paragraphs. Each sentence I write with intention. We all dream. But not equally. To make your dreams possible, act on them with open eyes.

5. I will realize life's true value.

Counting my days makes things of eternal value feel much more important. I am more aware than ever that my life is preparation for eternity. One day my heart will stop, and that will be the end of this body. But not the end of me.

Knowing that the quality of my life will never exceed the quality of my questions, I must ask outstanding questions. What am I doing that will count two hundred years from now? For eternity?

Present success or failure does not measure the true value of your life's work. You still have now.

Six words continue to motivate me: No reserves. No retreats. No regrets.

I am eternally grateful that YOU are in my life. The impact you have on me daily is beyond measure. What

Robert D. Smith

I do, what I think, who I am, and what I am becoming has been hugely influenced by you. For this I deeply and gratefully thank YOU!! I am so very proud of YOU and that God brought us together.

I look forward to counting more time with you and creating more memories that will truly last for all eternity.

Love you!!

TheRobertD

Robert D. Smith

"No reserves. No retreats. No regrets."

—William Borden
Christian missionary, heir to the Borden Inc. fortune
b. November 1, 1887, d. April 9, 1913
(He lived exactly 9,290 days)

The Little-Known Story of William Borden

Those six words—*No reserves. No retreats. No regrets*—made a huge impression on me. But wait until you've heard the story behind them.

William Borden was already wealthy when he graduated from a Chicago high school in 1904; he was the heir to his family's massive fortune. For his graduation present, William's parents gave him a trip that would take him around the world, to countries whose suffering he never could have imagined within the confines of his comfortable life.

At some point, as he traveled through Europe, the Middle East, and Asia, a simple burden began to grow heavy in his heart. He wanted to help these people who were far less fortunate than he had ever been.

At that moment, William decided to become a missionary once

he finished college. He wrote home, explaining his decision to family and friends.

When he finished his travels, he attended Yale, where he quickly distinguished himself from his typical peers. He started a small morning prayer group, and by his senior year, a thousand students were meeting in similar prayer groups inspired by his.

William's actions even reached beyond the campus. He founded the Yale Hope Mission in order to rehabilitate drunks forgotten on the streets of New Haven.

Given his family's position, he received numerous high-paying job offers after he finished his studies at Yale, but he turned them all down. After completing graduate work at Princeton Seminary, William sailed for Egypt, where he planned to learn Arabic before beginning his missions work in China. But while in Egypt, he was infected with spinal meningitis. The same month, William Borden died at the age of twenty-five.

The story of his life and death quickly made its way around American newspapers, capturing the attention of the entire country. His biographer, Mary Taylor, wrote, "A wave of sorrow went round the world… Borden not only gave his wealth, but himself, in a way so joyous and natural that it was manifestly a privilege rather than a sacrifice."

William's all-out dedication to making his life matter is reflected in a story that circulated after his death. According to the story, William had jotted down resolutions in the back of his Bible each time he faced key decisions in his life. The first, when he decided to become a missionary: "No reserves." The second, when he rejected the high-paying job offers: "No retreats." And the last, before his death: "No regrets."

No reserves. No retreats. No regrets.

William Borden made every day count. In the process of following his dream to become a missionary to the far corners of the world, he had a remarkable effect on those in his own community. He remained focused on his goal without losing sight of the here and now.

Did he reach his goal? No. But he fulfilled his purpose.

Before we can move forward and discuss how you, too, can truly live every day with purpose, we have to talk about a topic that is uncomfortable. Scary. Depressing. Taboo, even. *We have to talk about death.* Why? Because facing death, acknowledging it, and coming to terms with it is the best way to really live.

The next few chapters will explore the amazing, freeing perspective that comes from acknowledging our mortality. It's simple, attainable, and life-changing, and you can work it into your daily mind-set in positive, uplifting ways.

"*Dream as if you'll live forever.*
Live as if you'll die today."

—**James Dean**
American film actor
b. February 8, 1931, d. September 30, 1955
(He lived exactly 9,000 days)

Robert D. Smith

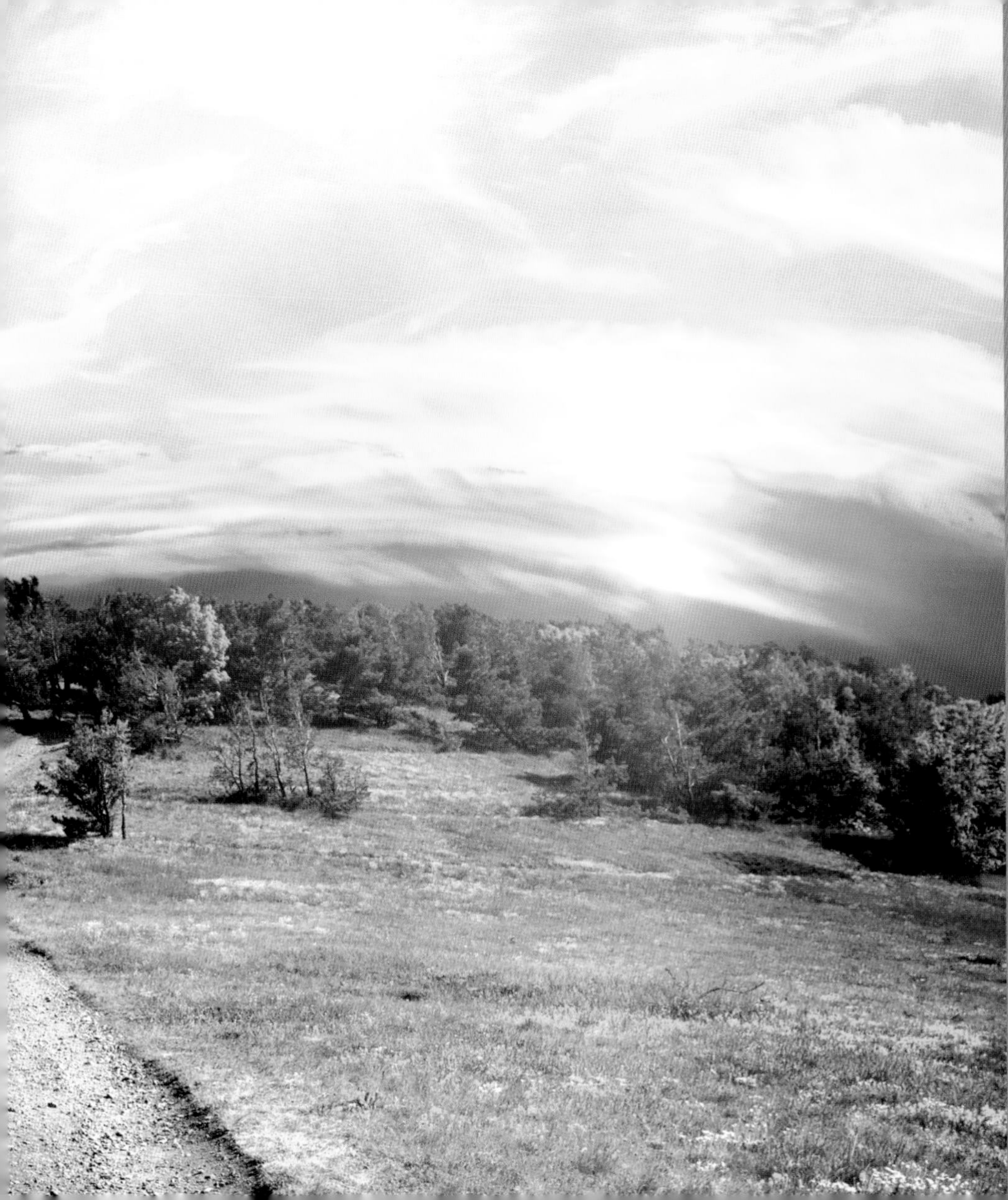

Living Each Day as If It Were Your Last

Whenever I read about someone who has passed away, I always count the years between the brackets. I suggest you do the same. James Dean was only twenty-four when he was killed in a car crash. I assure you, he did not plan on September 30, 1955, being his last day. But he could have, if he had lived as if it were.

I know that "live this day as if it were your last" is an old and tired cliché that is often written or spoken with little thought to it. But there's a reason why it is used so much. Let me explain.

The reality of that statement is this: if you were actually told that today was *your last day*, you'd waste hours trying to figure out exactly how you should be spending your final moments.

That's why "live this day as if it were your last" isn't about action. If it were about action, most people would blow off work

Robert P. Smith

and ignore 99 percent of their daily responsibilities, just trying to decide what to do. You wouldn't accomplish much for the long term. So it's not about actions. It's about mind-set. *It is a thought process*.

If it rained all day when you were expecting it to be sunny, would you be happy or a little bummed out? But what if it was the last time you were ever going to see it rain? You may see it as beautiful, because rain *is* beautiful. It grows life and sustains it for every living thing on the planet. And it smells like nothing else. Those rain-scented air fresheners and candles always disappoint me. They never come close to capturing it.

What about a paper cut? Would you complain about that sharp little pain or—if it were your last day—would you marvel at how your body will have practically healed it in just a few hours? It's all about eternal perspective.

Over thirty-five years ago, I read a book called *The Greatest*

Salesman in the World by a man named Og Mandino. It is a tiny book—a parable set in the time just before Christianity. It combines spirituality and mythology into a message of life-changing inspiration. The main character, a poor camel boy named Hafid, is given ten scrolls. Each scroll imparts critical wisdom and life principles, helping him achieve a life of abundance. The theme of the fifth scroll is "I will live this day as if it is my last." It is a couple of pages long and takes about five minutes to read.

Every day, for one month, I would read one of the scrolls aloud three times a day. I did this for five years. So, for one month a year during this five-year period, I would read the fifth scroll aloud to myself in the morning, afternoon, and evening. After doing that, it was kind of hard *not* to constantly have the last-day mind-set.

It is imperative that you get a copy of this book solely for the purpose of the fifth scroll. The whole book is amazing, but the fifth scroll will be of tremendous value to you.

Let's be frank. The reason why most people are unable to live with this mentality is that *it's tough*. It takes discipline, patience, and even courage because it requires you to live in a way that is contrary to how the majority of people around you are living their lives.

There are, however, three things you can do to make getting into this mind-set a little bit easier on yourself.

1. Create a Life Statement

Three simple sentences changed my life for thirty-five years. I discovered this little prayer while working with the Southwestern Publishing Company's summer program in 1975.

In this program, I was trained in life skills such as independence, confidence, self-motivation, and goal setting. I ran my own business selling educational books to families throughout the farmlands of Wisconsin.

I have said the following little prayer literally thousands of times. It has saved me from inactivity, helped me see how to overcome insurmountable obstacles, and catapulted me into massive action, a term I like to use that simply means accomplishing critical tasks rapidly. I have said this prayer every time I ever felt like I was at the end of my rope. It comes from *The Power of Positive Thinking* by Dr. Norman

Vincent Peale, which was first published in 1952, and it's still completely relevant and applicable today.

Hear it. Memorize it. Claim it. Make it yours this day and every day for the rest of your life:

I believe I am always divinely guided.
I believe I will always take the right turn in the road.
And I believe God will always make
a way where there is no way.

Do you see the power in this prayer? It literally covers any situation, problem, difficulty, setback, tragedy, or disaster that you will ever experience in life. Totally life encompassing!

Think of a challenge you are dealing with right now. One of these sentences directly addresses that challenge. It will give you hope and enable you to move forward with certainty. It's *that* powerful. Trust me.

2. Contact Important People

Which people matter most to you in life? Are there things you need to share with them? How can you express gratitude to them today? You can call or do something as simple as write a letter or an email.

Years ago, I wrote my mom and dad each a letter just to thank them for having me. That's an extraordinary concept we do not think about often enough. You and I would not be on this planet if our mothers and fathers had not given birth to us. It is a special bond that should never be forgotten, neglected, or undersold.

Even if you don't know your parents, have lost them or struggled with them, you can still write that letter of gratitude. Even if you can't or don't send it, it will still be a magical, healing, and empowering life experience. I promise.

Never forget the people who count in your life—not just

parents, but the other important people as well: teachers, mentors, spouses, friends, and more. Never forget what they've done for you. Honor them visibly. Let them know they matter and are critical to your life. Always.

Something occurred to me after talking to a highly sought-after speaker who receives a standing ovation almost every time he speaks: *Very few people on the planet will ever receive a standing ovation for anything they do in their entire lives.*

Suddenly, I took it upon myself to give everyone a standing ovation every day, every chance I could. It did not have to be a big deal. I knew I had to master celebrating the baby steps—the little accomplishments along the way—for myself and others.

At first, most people will not even know how to respond. But continue to celebrate. Soon others will join you in the celebration. Surprisingly, this seems to be one of those things that have to be learned and experienced.

Applaud everyone you can today. Step up and stand up! Yell loud and long. Celebrate who they are and who they are becoming.

3. **Number your days, daily**

You already know the story behind this one. Don't underestimate its power. Stop counting days down. Instead, count them up! Marvel at how many you've been allowed to spend on this planet. And never forget that each one could be your last.

There is no thought that will purge your priorities of worthless and worldly tastes like that of your impending death. Ponder the kind of life you would like to look back on when you come to die. There is enormous wisdom in such thoughts and meditation. Think often of your death. *It is essential to understand that you have been dying since the day you were born.*

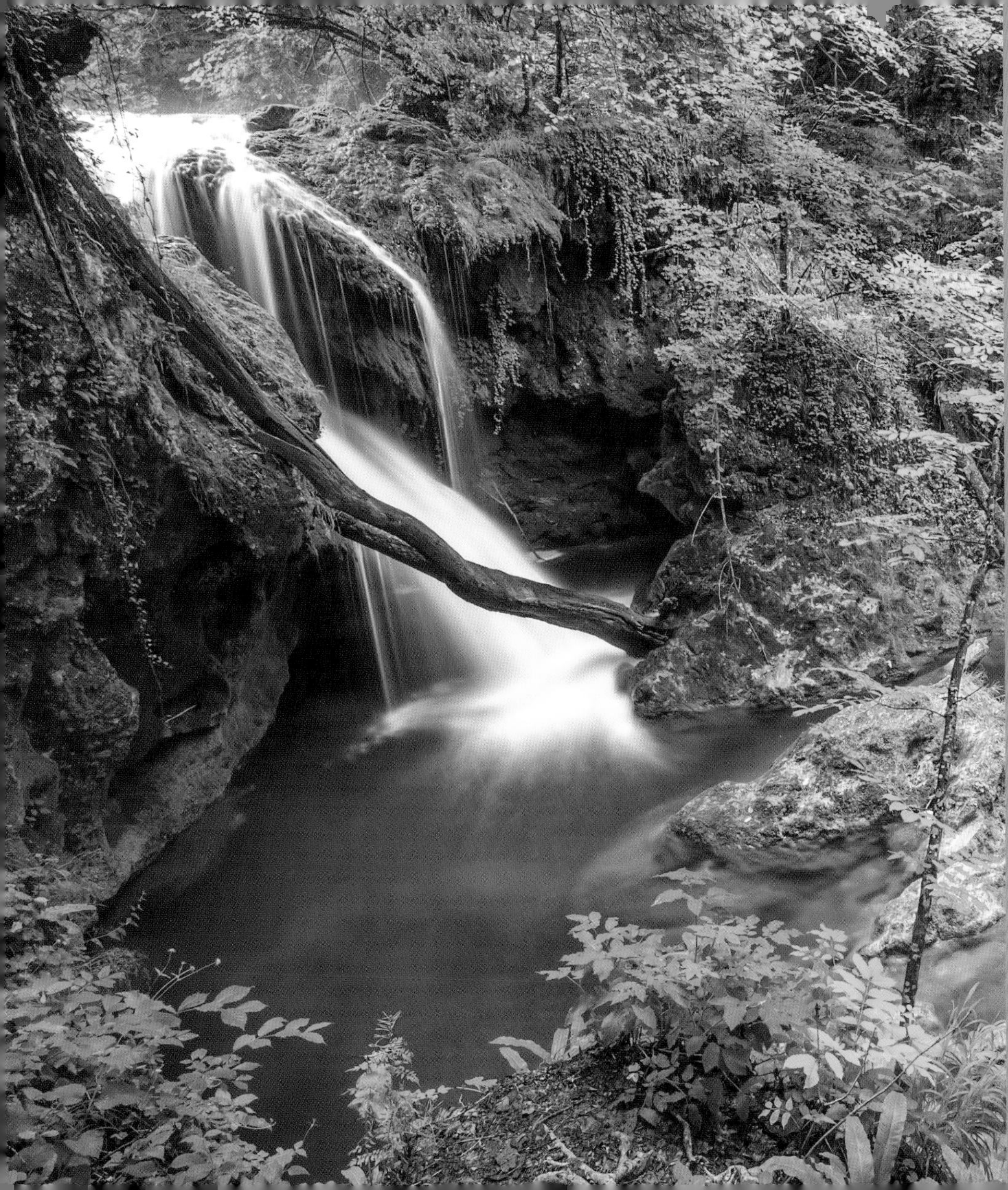

"One of the illusions [of life] is that the present hour is not the critical, decisive hour. Write it on your heart that every day is the best day in the year. No man has learned anything rightly until he knows that every day is Doomsday."

—Ralph Waldo Emerson
American essayist, lecturer, poet
b. May 25, 1803, d. April 27, 1882
(He lived exactly 28,827 days)

Robert P. Smith

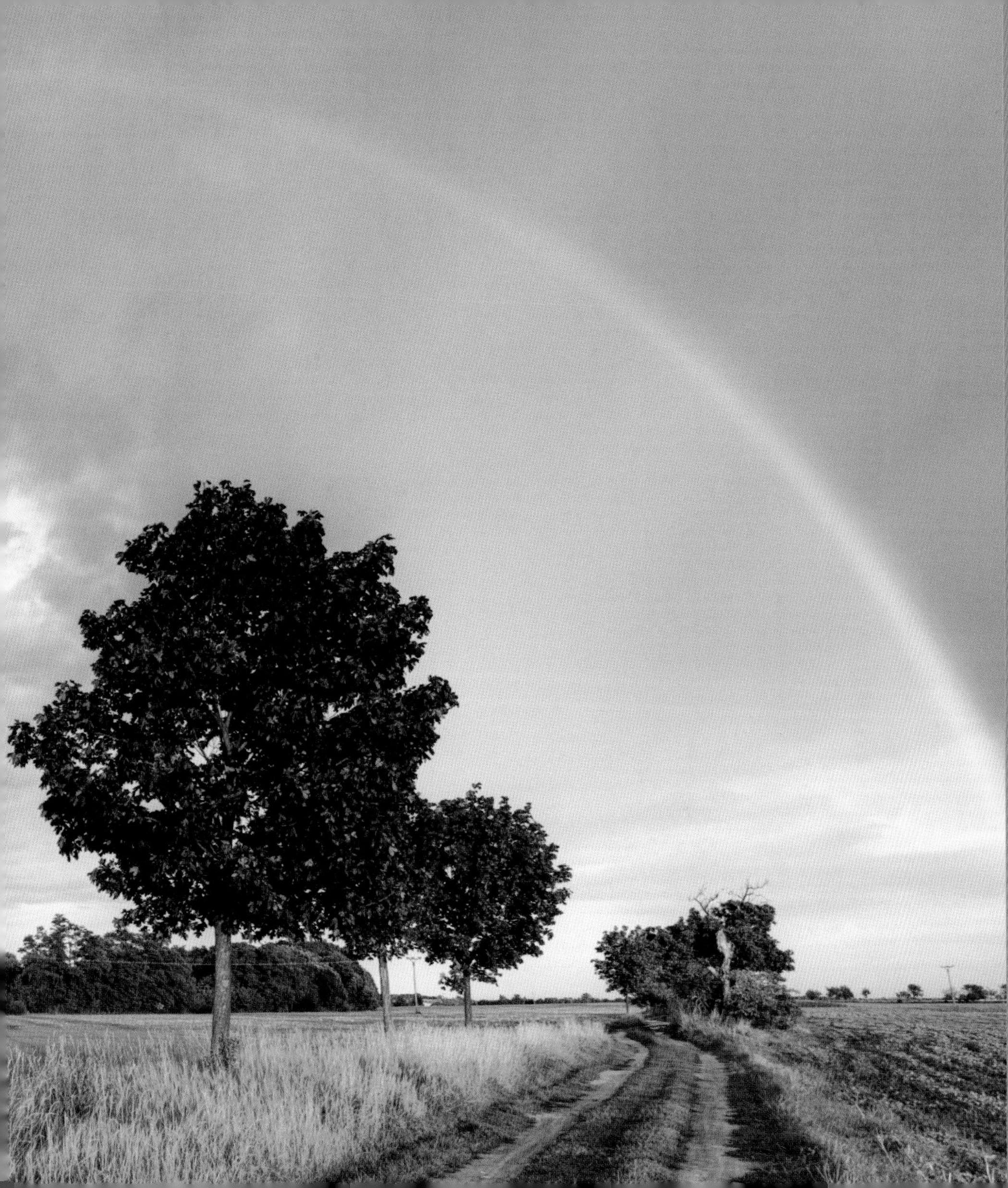

If We Can Learn How to Die, We'll Know How to Live

There are tens of thousands of self-help books on the market, thousands of hours of audio and video recordings to impart life wisdom, nonstop "how-to-live" YouTube videos, and entire TV networks devoted to inspiration. Never before in human history have so many people been ready to discover their purpose in life.

But you don't need a complicated system to get you on your way. It's simple, and by now you may have guessed. The best preparation for living well is to be *prepared* to die at any time. As we discussed, imminent death inspires clarity of purpose, a rearranging of what really matters. How many times have you heard of people having near-death experiences and then making radical changes in their lives? From where they live and work, to whom they spend time with, to what takes priority, it all suddenly has a different meaning.

Robert P. Smith

Whether it is a health scare or a terrifying plane ride, if you've ever waited for those test results to come back or for that turbulence to even out, those moments in between can feel like eternity. You question everything. And when you get the good news and the plane safely touches down, you are grateful and swear to live differently. *Why not pledge to live better right now?* Choose to be fully alive, purposeful, and loving today.

If we learn how to die, we'll know how to live; if we learn how to live, we'll know how to die.

I'm reminded of a short video I watched online called "When I Die: Lessons from the Death Zone." Google it; it's worth your time! It chronicles the inspiring last couple of weeks of a terminally ill man named Philip Gould. There is one thing in particular he says during the video that jumped out at me:

It's only when they say, "Philip Gould, you're going to die. Get used to it. And this is going to happen in weeks or months." It's only when that happens that you're aware of death. And it's only when that happens that suddenly life screams at you with its intensity.

I want you to read that last part again: "suddenly life screams at you with its intensity."

We all have an amazing ability to overlook the intensity of our everyday lives. We get wrapped up in what we mistakenly call the mundane, the grind, the everydayness of life.

In the classic Walker Percy novel *The Moviegoer*, the main character, Binx Bolling, claims to be on a loosely defined "search" in life. "What is the nature of the search?" he asks in the book. "The search is what anyone would undertake if he were not sunk in the everydayness of his own life."

What are you searching for? Maybe it's a search for meaning, for an answer, for a solution to a problem you know you're equipped to solve. What is standing in the way of your search? Are you getting so bogged down in the day-to-day minutiae of your life that you overlook the power of each moment? Your search is your purpose. Remind yourself of it daily. Remember that it's the little things that add up to the big picture. Do not wait for impending death to light the fire of action inside yourself. Act today. Start small. There are opportunities hiding in the "day-to-day."

How long does it take to discover your purpose in life? Believe it or not, twenty minutes! Remember, we are short on time, so we have to hurry. So be open to this. You must expect it to work; then it will.

1. **Get a blank sheet of paper. Title it "My Purpose in Life."**

2. **Start writing. Right now. Write. Write all you can. Words, phrases, complete sentences. Just write. Don't stop. Write some more.**

3. **Repeat step two until you get the answer that makes you either cry or jump up and down with excitement. Condense it into one sentence. This is your purpose.**

Here is my purpose, condensed down to one sentence:

The purpose of my life is to touch hearts that are hurting, enjoy laughter, and create permanent abundance for others and myself in a most joyful and playful way while feeling like a "giggle."

Discovering your purpose may be the easy part. The hard part is keeping it in front of you daily to the point where it drives you continuously.

This Native American proverb sums it up best: "When you were born, you cried and the world rejoiced. Live your life so that when you die, the world cries and you rejoice."

Robert D. Smith

"*A day wasted on others is not wasted on one's self.*"

—**Charles Dickens**
British novelist
b. February 7, 1812, d. June 9, 1870
(He lived exactly 21,307 days)

The State of Intensity

Many people may think that intensity is a state of mind. But it is not. Intensity is a state of emotion. Intensity goes from the heart to the head. Intensity is enthusiasm. Intensity is passion. Intensity is being in love. You have to be emotionally connected to what you are doing in order to pursue it with intensity.

If you are playing a game of golf and you simply don't care about the outcome, your intensity will be low. Your focus will be weak. Your performance will be mediocre. However, if you are playing any game and something important to you is on the line (money, title, reputation, pride), everything changes.

For example, let's say you're playing a game of golf where the winner will receive a valuable prize: money, an award, or recognition. Now, all of a sudden, the players are emotionally

Robert D. Smith

engaged. They care about the outcome. They are focused on the reward, and their intensity goes up twentyfold.

In order to make every day count, *you must have that emotional connection*—the fanatical commitment to follow through. Most likely you have already created that desire, the intensity, the passion that will pull you forward. Now it's just a matter of tapping into it on a consistent basis. Deep down, you know what counts in life. Simply focus on it.

"*Time goes, you say? Ah no!
Alas, Time stays, we go.*"

—**Henry Austin Dobson**
British author
b. January 18, 1840, d. September 2, 1921
(He lived exactly 29,812 days)

Robert D. Smith

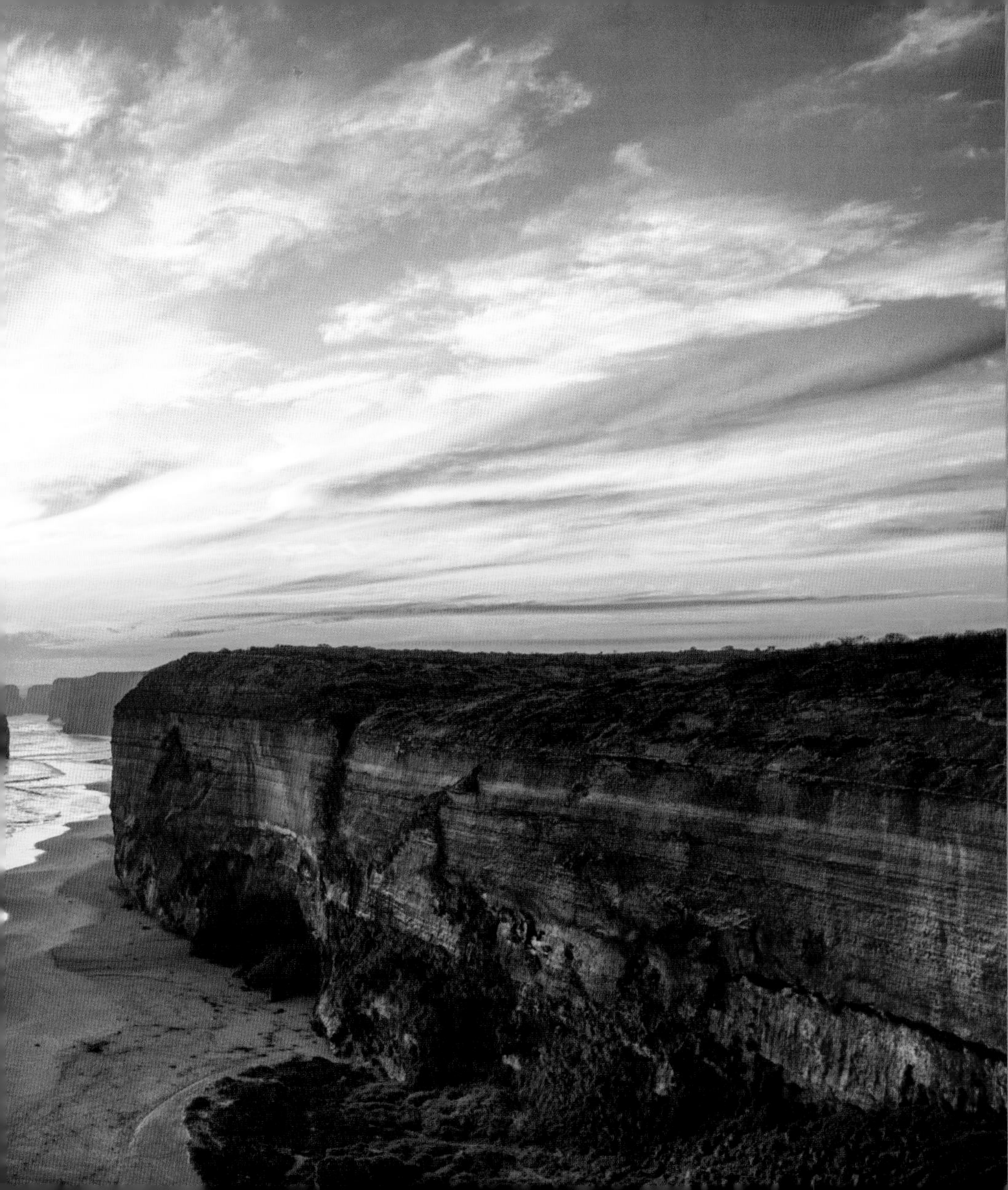

Eat Dessert First

You know when you're out to dinner and that really amazing, decadent dessert on the menu catches your eye? You file it away in your mind and think, *I'll get that after the meal.* Then, by the time you're done and it's time for dessert, you're too full to eat anything else! Sound familiar?

Celebrating your life is kind of like that. We always think, *Now's not the time to stop and celebrate. I'll do that once I've (insert lofty goal you want to accomplish here).*

Here's the problem with that philosophy: if you don't stop to celebrate the little steps along the way, you get burned out! You get "too full," just like when you put off dessert. That's why, if you ever happen to go out to dinner with me, I always insist on everyone ordering dessert *first.* I'm talking before the appetizers even come out.

Order the dessert before you have time to fill up, before you have time to think about the calories. You can work those off! These are similar to the excuses we try to use for *not* celebrating: "I don't have time. I'm too tired. I haven't accomplished anything major yet."

Forget about those excuses. The little steps must be recognized and honored. The main goal would be unreachable without them.

Don't even wait for the opportunity to arise. At dinner, if you wait for the other people at the table to mention dessert, chances are, they won't. They're sitting there hoping YOU will mention it!

Life is the same way. Life is waiting on you. Celebrate for simply waking up in the morning. Turn on some fun music. Dance! Jump up and down when you get out of bed. Spreading celebration and joy is the only way to withstand the intensity of your mission. Remember this as you read on. I can't wait for you to see what comes next. There is much work to be done and much to be celebrated!

But just for a moment, stop here. Celebrate yourself getting this far!

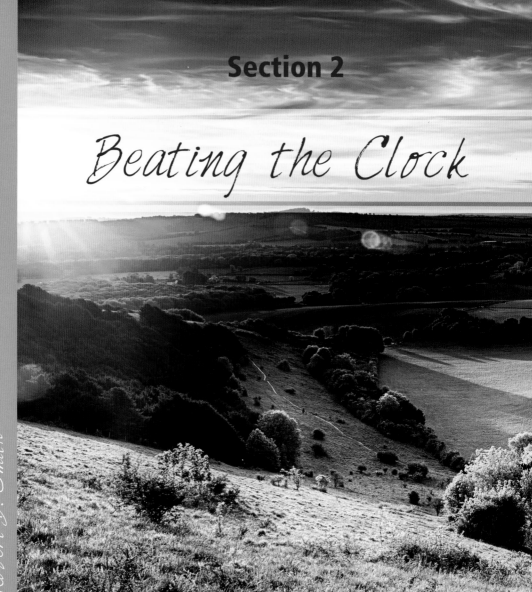

Section 2

Beating the Clock

Robert D. Smith

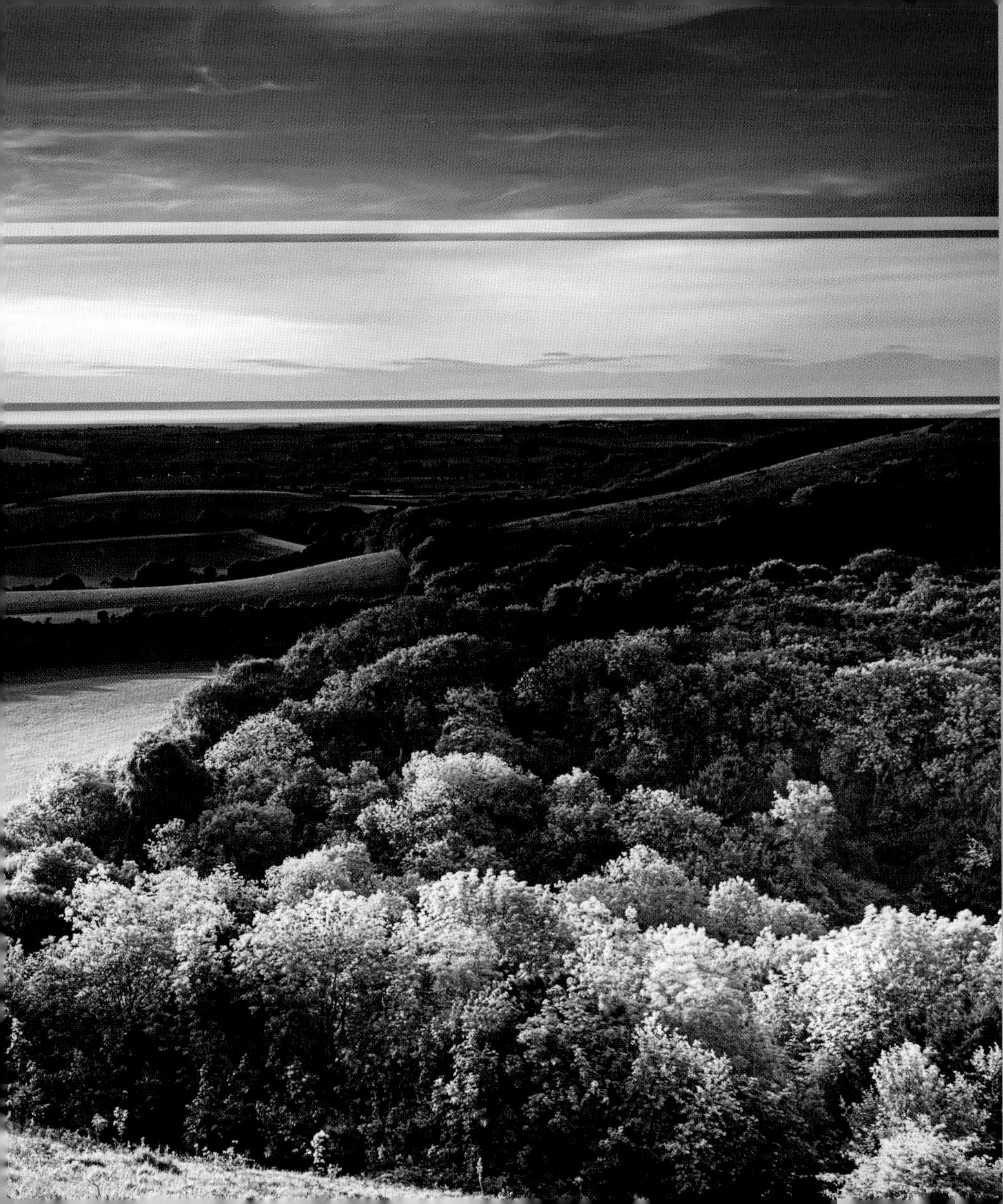

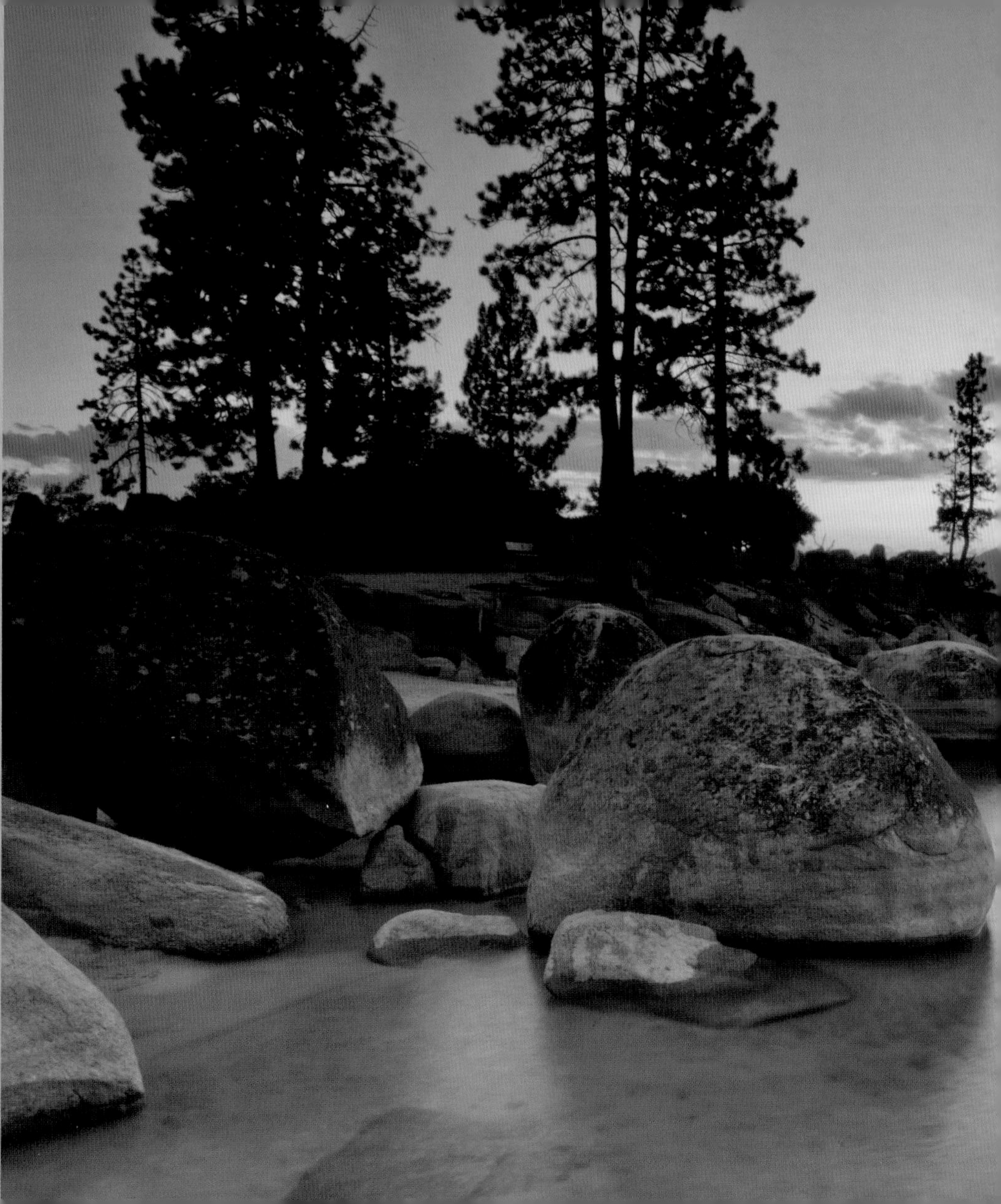

Robert D. Smith

"**A man who dares to waste one hour of his time has not discovered the value of life.**"

—**Charles Darwin**
British naturalist
b. February 12, 1809, d. April 19, 1882

(He lived exactly 26,729 days)

Motivation Is a Myth

You may hear people saying all the time, "Take action!" "Do something!" "Do better!" We all know how difficult it can be to get someone to make a move, especially ourselves. But how do you get yourself—or anyone else—to do it?

Let me give you a hint: it's definitely not a question of motivation. Why? Because motivation is a myth.

Believe me. You cannot motivate people to do any one thing. Even yourself. Never try to motivate yourself or anyone else to increase productivity. Instead, do the opposite:

Increase your productivity, then the motivation will follow.

We are always trying to get ourselves to find a better or more efficient way to do things instead of getting ourselves excited to do better. But when we actually *do* better, we get excited, and the cycle continues!

I always feel better after I do what I am supposed to do, not before. Beforehand, there is always a little bit of nervousness and hesitation, along with thoughts like *What are people going to say?* and *Can I do this?* But afterward, I always feel great. I've accomplished something.

Exercising is a prime example. I have never *wanted* to work out in my life—but I am *always* glad I did. What about being creative? I have a close friend who is a successful author. He says he hates to write—but he is always elated once he has written. Sound familiar?

We know what we are supposed to be doing, but when we wait for that motivation to come ahead of time, it never does. The reason is because we have it backward.

Psychologist William James believed that we don't sing because we're happy; we're happy because we sing. I really love this idea. Believe it and *sing*! In the shower if you have to. Sing while you *do something*, and infuse it with joy. It beats waiting around for inspiration any day.

"The hours of folly are measured by the clock, but of wisdom no clock can measure."

—**William Blake**
British poet, painter
b. November 28, 1757, d. August 12, 1827
(He lived exactly 25,458 days)

Robert P. Smith

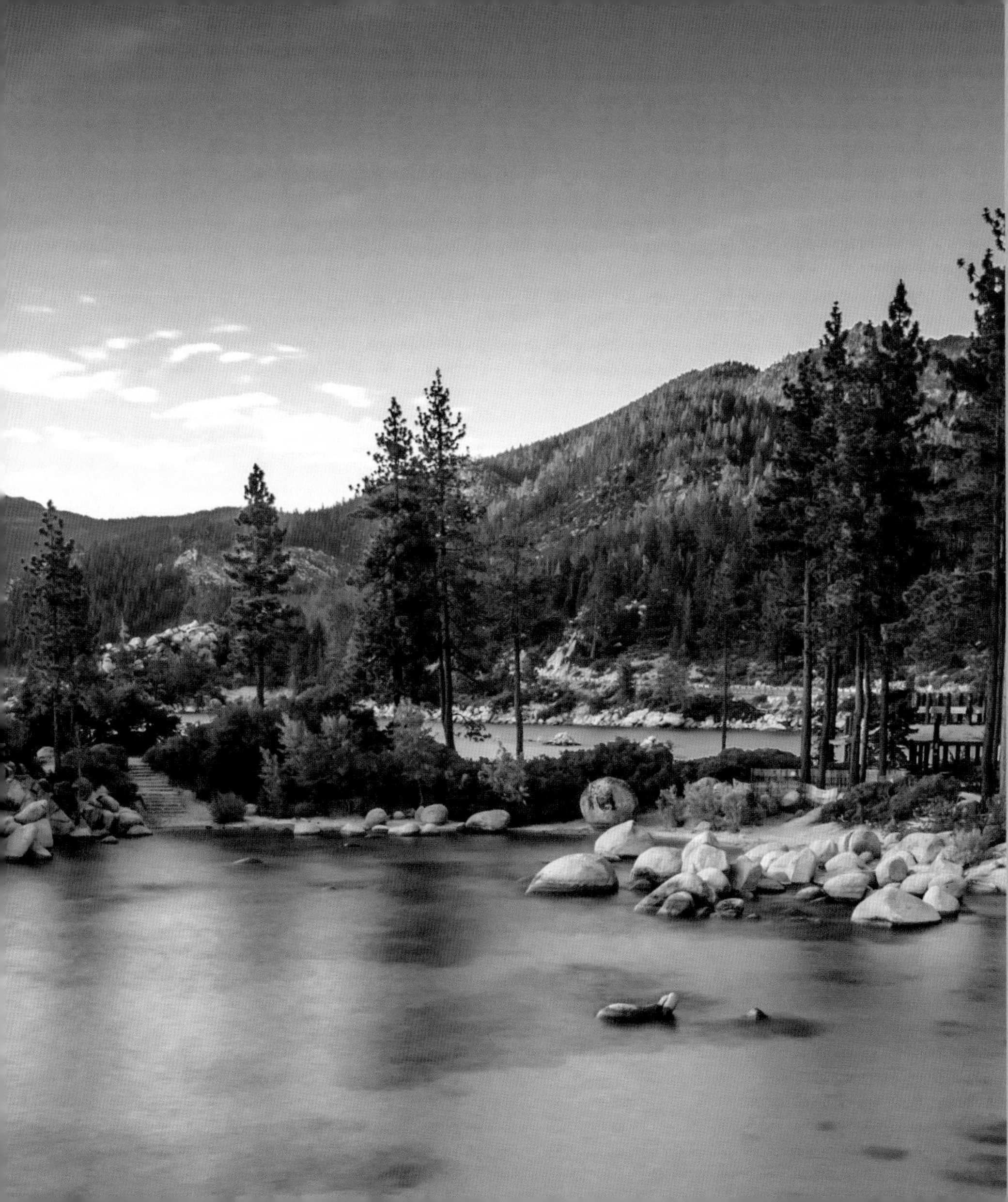

You Only Have Two Choices

As I was thinking of a way to explain exactly what it takes to really move forward with your life and to live beyond your wildest dreams, I realized how simple it is. But simple is not the same as easy.

For instance, think about how many books are published every year or how much publishing is done daily in newspapers and magazines and online, despite the fact that there are only twenty-six letters in our alphabet. Those few little symbols make up all the words we have, and they create an incredibly complex form of communication.

It is the same way with numbers. Think of all the money you made today—and all the money you didn't make. Think of your personal debt. Think of how many billions of dollars are being made by big corporations. And yet there are only ten digits in our numerical system.

And then there are colors. Think of all the different colors there are to choose from. Just try to decide on a paint color, or more specifically, a shade. I recently saw an entire book of paint chips for the color white. White! Is that even a color? I wanted white drapes, and the interior decorator brought me an entire book of whites. So many shades, and yet there are only three primary colors from which all colors come: red, blue, and yellow.

I could go on and on with examples. But here's the point: Of all the decisions we have to make every day, how many real choices do you have? *There are only two.* That's right, just TWO.

You only can decide *yes* or *no.* How simple is that? But not always easy.

In everyday situations, you are faced with yes-or-no scenarios all day long. They may be masked as something more complicated, but really, it's fifty-fifty.

This is where little actions add up to big ones. Constantly saying *no*—to lunch, to that project, to a vacation, to whatever it may be—diminishes opportunities for discovery and growth. If you want things to change in your life, you have to be open to change, to new possibilities. To *yes*.

Ask yourself this question: *Who do I have to become to achieve (fill in the blank)?* What's your desired outcome? I guarantee that 99.9 percent of the time this will involve becoming someone who is willing to say *yes* more often.

If you choose *no*, you might say, "No, I don't have control of my life or my destiny." "No, I don't really have time to pursue my goals." "No, I don't care for tomorrow because I'm living just for today." No goals, no direction, no ambition—therefore, no vision and no hope. As a rule, *noes* do *not* move you forward.

Or you could say YES! "Yes, I have decided to enjoy my life today." "Yes, I want to do the best I can." "Yes, I want to give my family the best." "Yes, I want to do the best at my work, and I want to be the very best I can." Yes, you can decide YES! You can continue to pursue your goals and your dreams.

Here is where it gets tricky. It's not always easy to say *yes*. *Yes* means taking chances, putting yourself out there, embracing the unknown. But when you open yourself up to *yes*, amazing opportunities, exciting possibilities, and good results come your way. Marvelous memories are created. You expand your territory and that of others.

What challenge can you own and say *yes* to right now? As Yoda put it in *The Empire Strikes Back*, "Do or do not; there is no try."

"*Take time by the forelock. Now or never! You must live in the moment, launch yourself on every wave, find your eternity in each moment.*"

—Henry David Thoreau
American writer
b. July 12, 1817, d. May 6, 1862
(He lived exactly 16,369 days)

Robert D. Smith

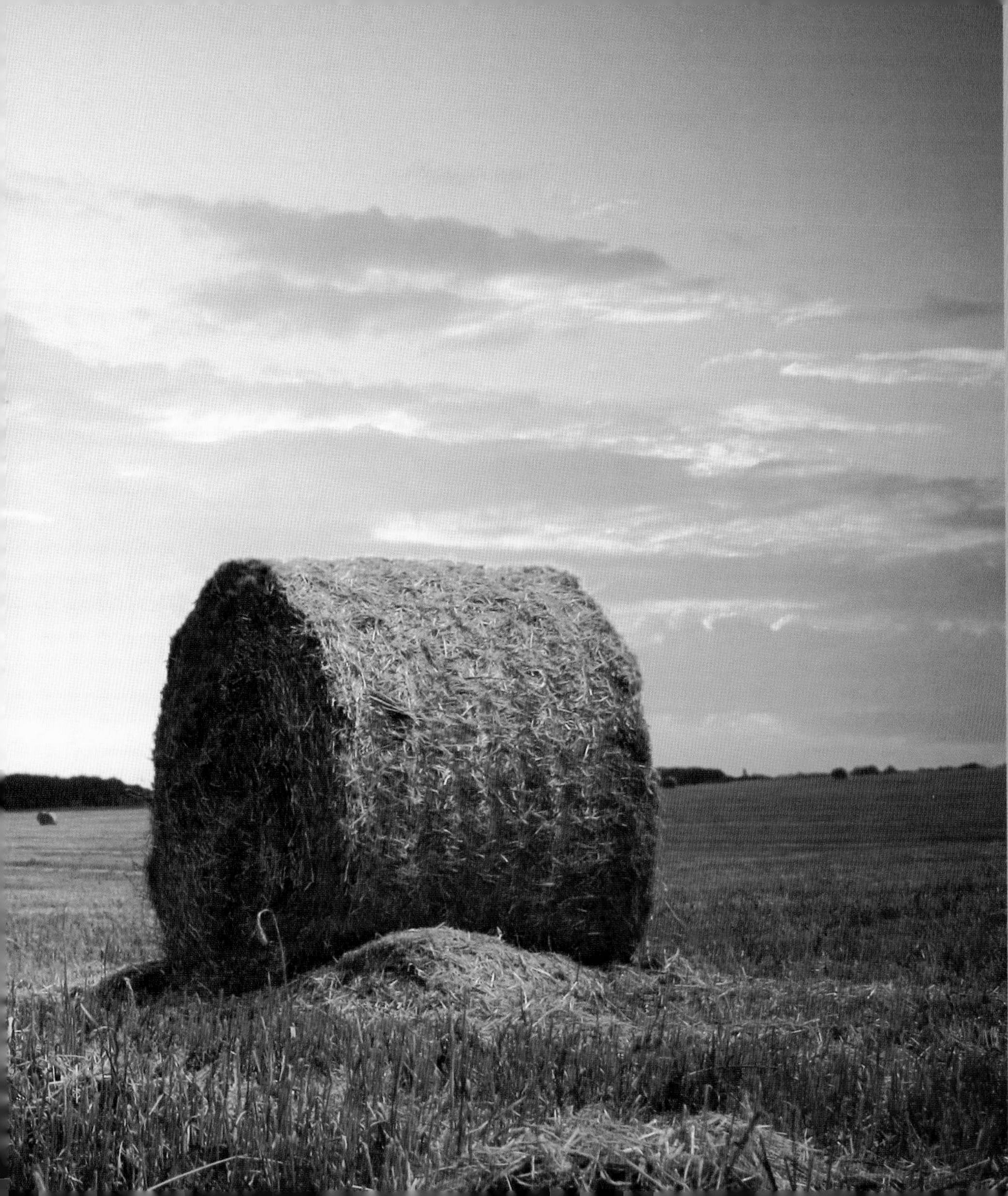

The Real Challenge

I was thinking the other day about one of my all-time favorite heroes, Sherlock Holmes. I've always liked the way he analyzes every single crime. His forte is asking the questions that nobody else is asking, questions like, "What if there were two murderers instead of one?" It is amazing how the police chief was always so surprised!

You know what? Sherlock never had to prove there were two murderers; he only had to ask the question, and doors were opened. He takes the same evidence everyone has and looks at it in a new way.

The same thing can be applied to our lives, although hopefully not because we're trying to solve a murder! We all have our own individual problems, but if we put on our Sherlock Holmes hats, ask questions, and look at them from different perspectives, we may find those problems are self-imposed.

Robert D. Smith

What if I told you there is a simple way to solve *all* your problems by changing just one aspect of your thought process? Sounds too good to be true, right? But let me tell you a story that shows how it works.

After college, I volunteered at the Crisis Center, a mental health agency in Birmingham, Alabama, for a couple years. People in crisis would call the help line, and we would serve them as best we could. We were taught to deal with just the individual caller. We weren't supposed to deal with a spouse, brother, sister, mother, or father. It was only the caller. We phrased our questions directly toward that person: "What can *you* do? What do *you* think? How do *you* feel about this?"

We found this to be very powerful when dealing with emergency situations. But the thing is, it gives rise to the one idea that can change *everything* for you. Ready for it?

Become your own problem.

Yes, you read that right! This may be tough for you perfectionists, but stay with me. Start thinking, *I am the problem. I am the problem. I am the problem.* When you do that, you take the outside circumstances and bring them inside. Suddenly, you have power.

If you assume that you are the victim, you lose power. You shut down all creativity. But when you bring it inside yourself, now the ball is in your court and you can do something about it. *You* have control. See the switch?

Remember, it is a thinking process, not a feeling process. Some people may say, "Well, I don't want to be the problem. That feels very negative." But it's not. It is really good news! If you're the problem, you can solve it. So assume the responsibility, own the difficulty, and I guarantee you will create a solution.

What one struggle are you thinking of right now that you would love to magically solve? You are about to solve it.

Play along…

If you were transported one year into the future, looking back, how would you advise yourself right now?

How can YOU become the problem in this situation?

Now that YOU are the problem, what changes will you make?

Step away from the situation. Think with your head. Don't feel with your heart. Be honest.

I know you just came up with the solution! Now act on it.

> **"The first hour of the morning is the rudder of the day."**
>
> —**Henry Ward Beecher**
> American preacher, orator, writer
> b. June 24, 1813, d. March 8, 1887
> **(He lived exactly 26,920 days)**

Robert P. Smith

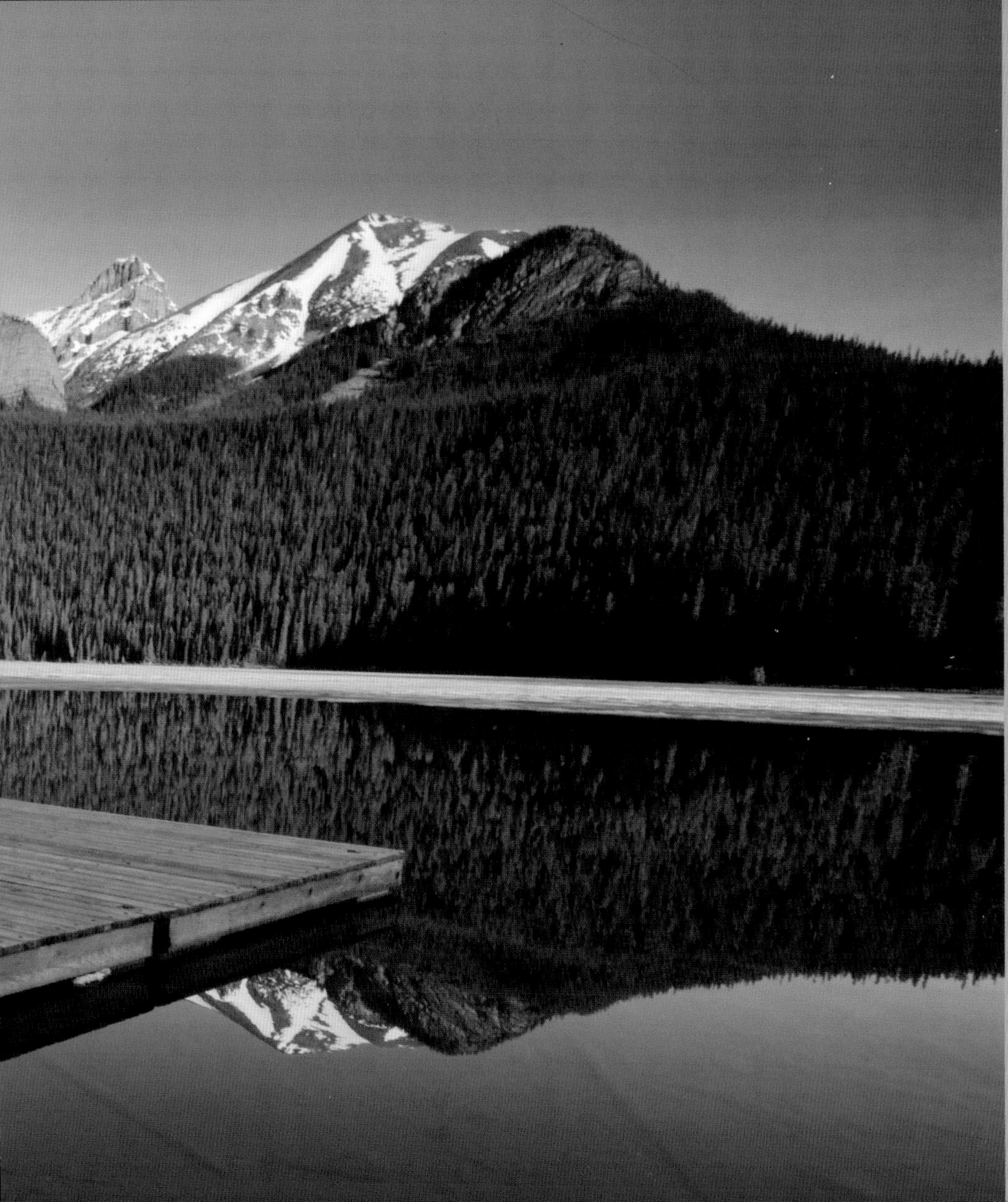

Focusing Your Morning Vision

How do you start your day? What matters most when you're fresh out of bed? Here is what a typical morning thought process is like for me:

1. **When I first open my eyes, I immediately feel grateful and full of anticipation. This is a new day. I have more chances, opportunities, and unexpected privileges because I stepped up and took responsibility in all areas of my life.**

2. **I rise quickly. I quickly act the way I want to feel, overriding whatever feelings may have overtaken me during the night. I have mastered the ability to reach an immediate peak state when I open my eyes.**

3. **I focus on my number one priority of the day:** meditation. **I prioritize my daily list of things to do by what's most important and rewarding, well before I start. I purposely find ways to spend more time each day on what's most important to me.**

4. **I will not fail to deliver on God's mission for my life. I mean to make myself a man after God's own heart. If I succeed in that, I will succeed in everything else.**

I know; it's intense. But that's how life is meant to be lived—intensely. And I guarantee that waking up with that kind of attitude will do a hundred times what any cup of coffee could ever do.

This day is a gift. Greet it that way.

"Take care of the things you need to take care of today."

—Horace
Roman poet
b. December 8, 65 BC, d. November 27, 8 BC
(He lived exactly 20,830 days)

Robert P. Smith

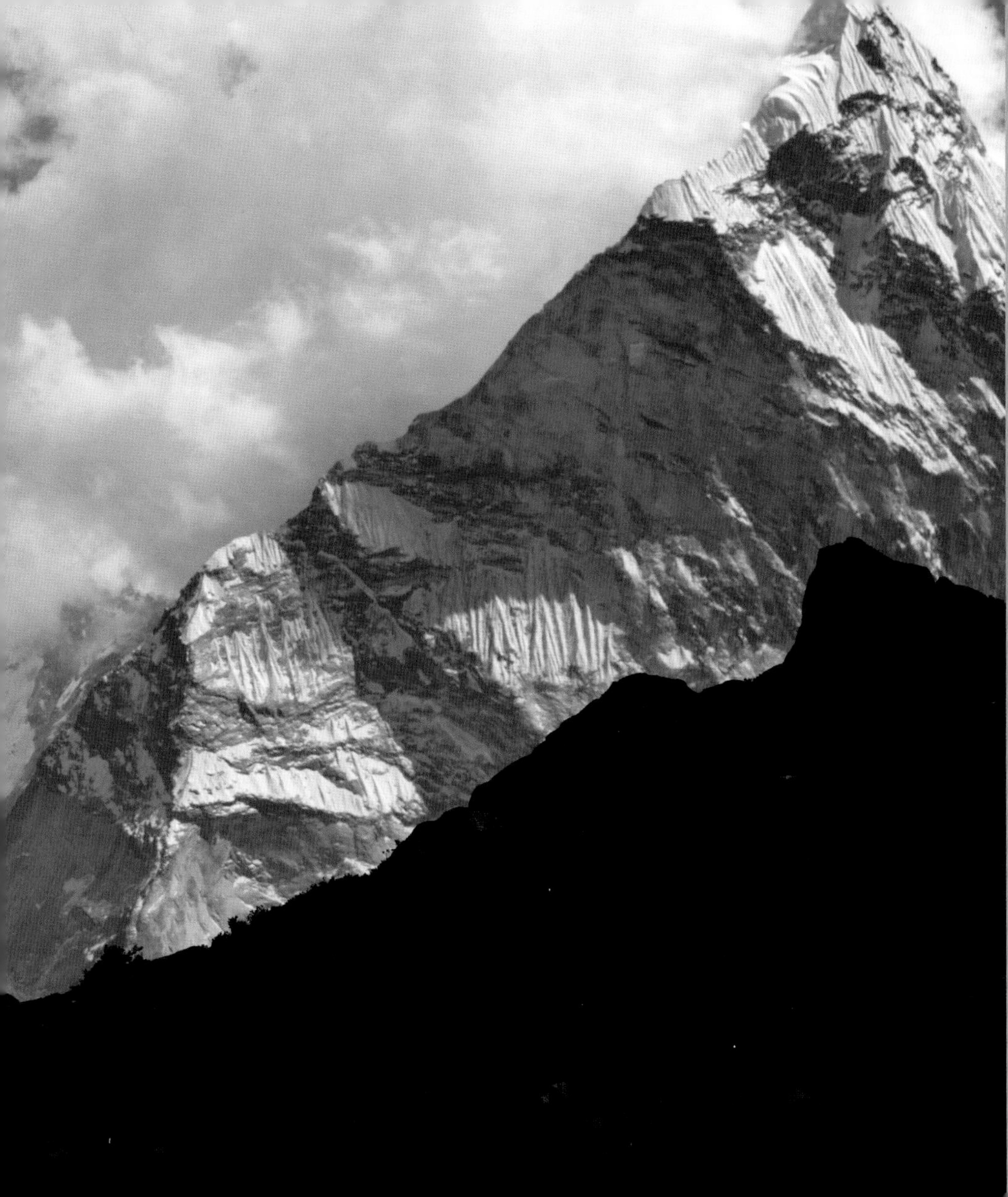

Doing What You Know

We talked about how time passes much more quickly than we expect. Always. Christmas seems to come faster than ever now. The weekend, Monday, deadlines in general, are all coming faster and faster. Time seems to be spinning into a black hole.

Yet, when it comes to your dreams, your career, time can seem like it's grinding to a halt.

I know that sometimes I sit down and think, *What do I do next? What am I supposed to do next? What have I got to do next?*

For a moment I freeze and think, *I don't know. I absolutely don't have a clue.* Then I realize that I do.

Anybody who has gone through a day of school—and we all have—knows what to do next. School is structured, scheduled. There is always something coming up.

Robert D. Smith

So, when faced with the question of what's next, *do what you know to do.*

Think of something you want to accomplish and focus on that. It is that thing you are thinking of right now. It's the thing that is crossing your mind: *If I would only do this one thing.* Just do all you can, and that is all you can accomplish in a day. If you do that on a daily basis, your life will change.

Herb Kelleher, founder of Southwest Airlines, gave an inside glimpse of what made him successful: "We do have a strategic plan. It's called doing things."

Somehow the pieces of the puzzle always come together. So when you hit a wall and don't know what to do, *do* what you know to do.

"One can always trust to time. Insert a wedge of time and nearly everything straightens itself out."

— **George Norman Douglas**
British author
b. December 8, 1868, d. February 7, 1952
(He lived exactly 30,375 days)

Robert P. Smith

How to Conquer Rejection Forever

Rejection is a part of life that we have been trained to find unpleasant. But what if every rejection only meant you were one step closer to a *yes*? What if you considered rejection to be a crucial part of your search instead of an obstacle? What if it were merely a chapter in the much larger story of your purpose?

That's the mind-set I had when I sold books door-to-door for Southwestern back in college. If there's one profession where you'll learn a lot about rejection, it's door-to-door sales.

Here's the part that made dealing with rejection easy: my goal was not to sell a single book. I didn't care about the sale. All I cared about was doing thirty presentations every single day. Even if I got thirty *noes*, I still would have accomplished my goal.

But the interesting thing is, I never got thirty *noes* in a row. If I did my presentation so many times in one day, there was at least one person (sometimes more) who would inevitably give me a *yes*.

Years later, I applied this same principle when I was trying to get bookings for Andy Andrews, the comedian I was representing. My goal was to get him into the college market, so every day I would sit down with a telephone (this was decades before the Internet) and cold call at least thirty colleges.

I would actually ask, "You wouldn't be interested in booking a comedian, would you?" Remember, I was looking for thirty colleges a day that did *not* want a comedian. Obviously, the *yes* would change the outcome of the game, but, in my mind, I was always hunting for *noes*. That is where the production came from. Ultimately, I would always find my one *yes* after wading through a sea of *noes*. Never once did I ever succeed in getting thirty *noes* in a row.

It wasn't long before he was the most booked comedian in the college market, and voted Comedian of the Year for two years in a row by the National Association for Campus Activities (NACA). It became a platform that pushed him into the national spotlight.

So *noes* do not intimidate me. I eat *noes* for breakfast.

So often, I have friends come up to me and lament about their inability to accomplish some kind of goal, like publishing a book. When I ask them how many times they've been turned down, they usually respond with nothing greater than three or four. They take those three or four rejections as evidence that they should give up. That's when I give them the good news: they're just getting started!

That same comedian I was booking all those years ago eventually wrote a book. It was called *The Traveler's Gift*. As his manager and someone who greatly believed in the book, I was responsible for finding a publisher. You know how many publishers completely rejected it? Fifty-one. That's right, fifty-one publishers told me that what he had written was not worth putting on paper.

But you know what happened after we finally found our *yes*?

The book got published, became a featured selection on *Good Morning America* and a *New York Times* bestseller, was translated into over twenty-five languages, and launched Andy Andrews's writing career. He has since authored many more books, including multiple *New York Times* bestsellers.

What would have happened if Andy and I had given up after three or four *noes*?

What have you given up on? What do you want so badly that you would pitch it to thirty people who will tell you *no*? What are you eating for breakfast? Go get yourself a big bowl of *noes*! You will be shocked at how big and strong you will grow.

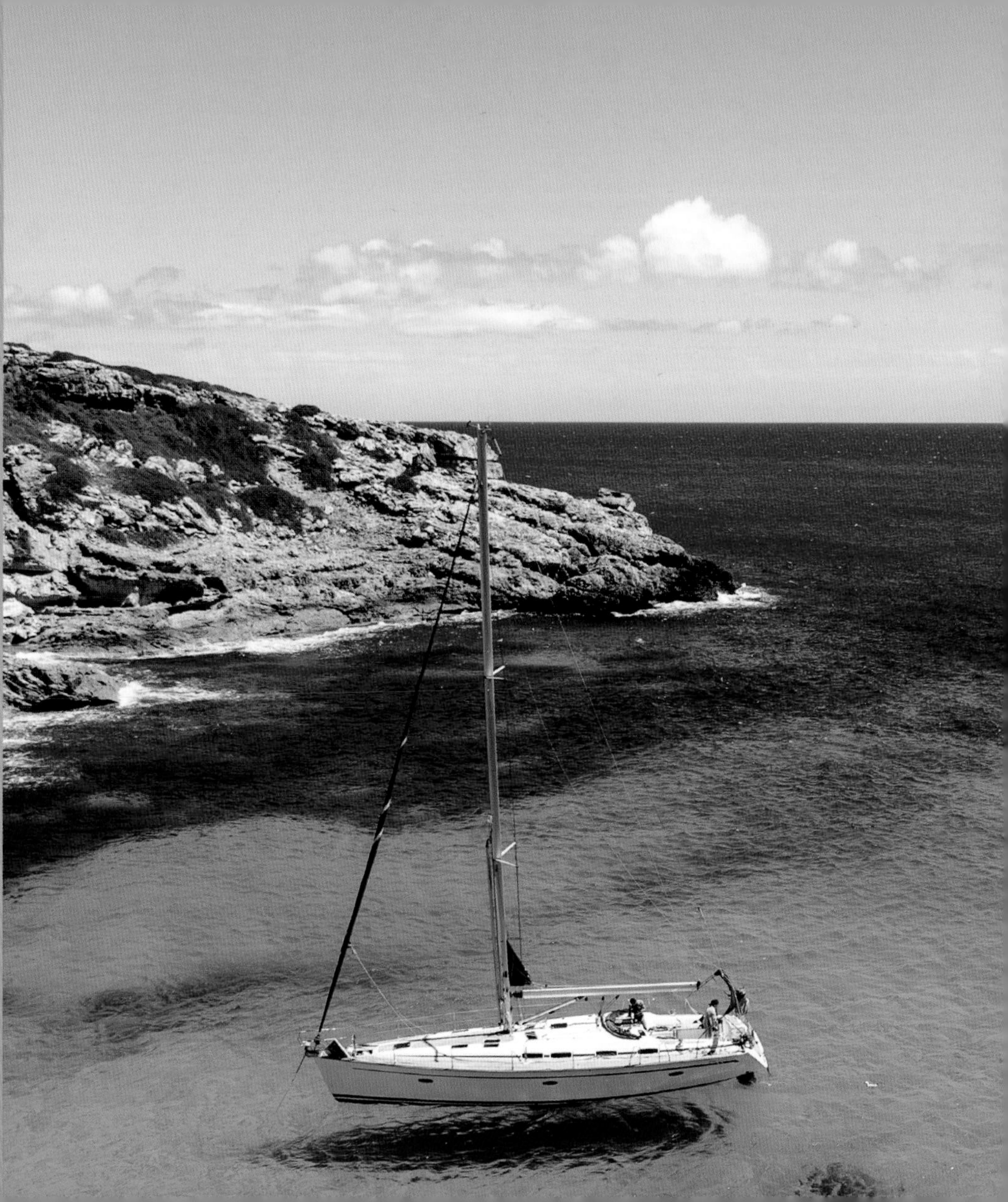

Robert D. Smith

"You never will find time for anything. If you want time, you must make it."

—**Charles Buxton**
British author
b. November 18, 1823, d. August 10, 1871
(He lived exactly 17,432 days)

Ripples

Time. The process. The plan. Agenda.

Are you spending life merely reacting to events as they happen, or are you moving forward each day with a clear objective? When you form a clear plan for your life, every day becomes part of something bigger: the process. It's up to you, however, to determine who you are in the process of becoming.

So how do you become a planner? Become a process fanatic. Love the activity. List what you have thought about and what you are to become. Your life will take place whether you have a plan or not, so have a plan. Choose one. Say *yes*! Make one up. Design it. Put in all the detail you want. Who is in it? Where does it take place? Fill in specifics, even how much money you make. (I love that one.)

You are the pebble that has been dropped into this gorgeous, beautiful, incredible, God-made, awe-inspiring pool of life. The pebble knows not of the ripples it creates. But there are always incalculable numbers of ripples that go to the edge of eternity. And you simply float to the bottom of the pool. But it's not just the bottom; it's the foundation. It is the foundation of everything you are. It is everything you are to become. It is everything you are creating.

But you don't stay on the bottom for long. Because somehow, during the night, you are plucked from the bottom, brought up out of the water, and dropped again. It starts all over. Daily. Sometimes you are dropped several times a day. Over a period of time, the pool gets bigger and deeper. You, the rock, get bigger too. The ripples are bigger and farther reaching. They can and may actually become waves, reaching many more people.

Every day you have an opportunity to make ripples. You never really cross the finish line. Performing at a big show, publishing a book, or even getting a record deal isn't the finish line. It's the new starting line. Every day you can say to yourself: *Now the real work begins.*

This is not a quick makeover. This is a process. Winning is defined by the legacy you create, and legacies always take time to build.

Now, let's start building.

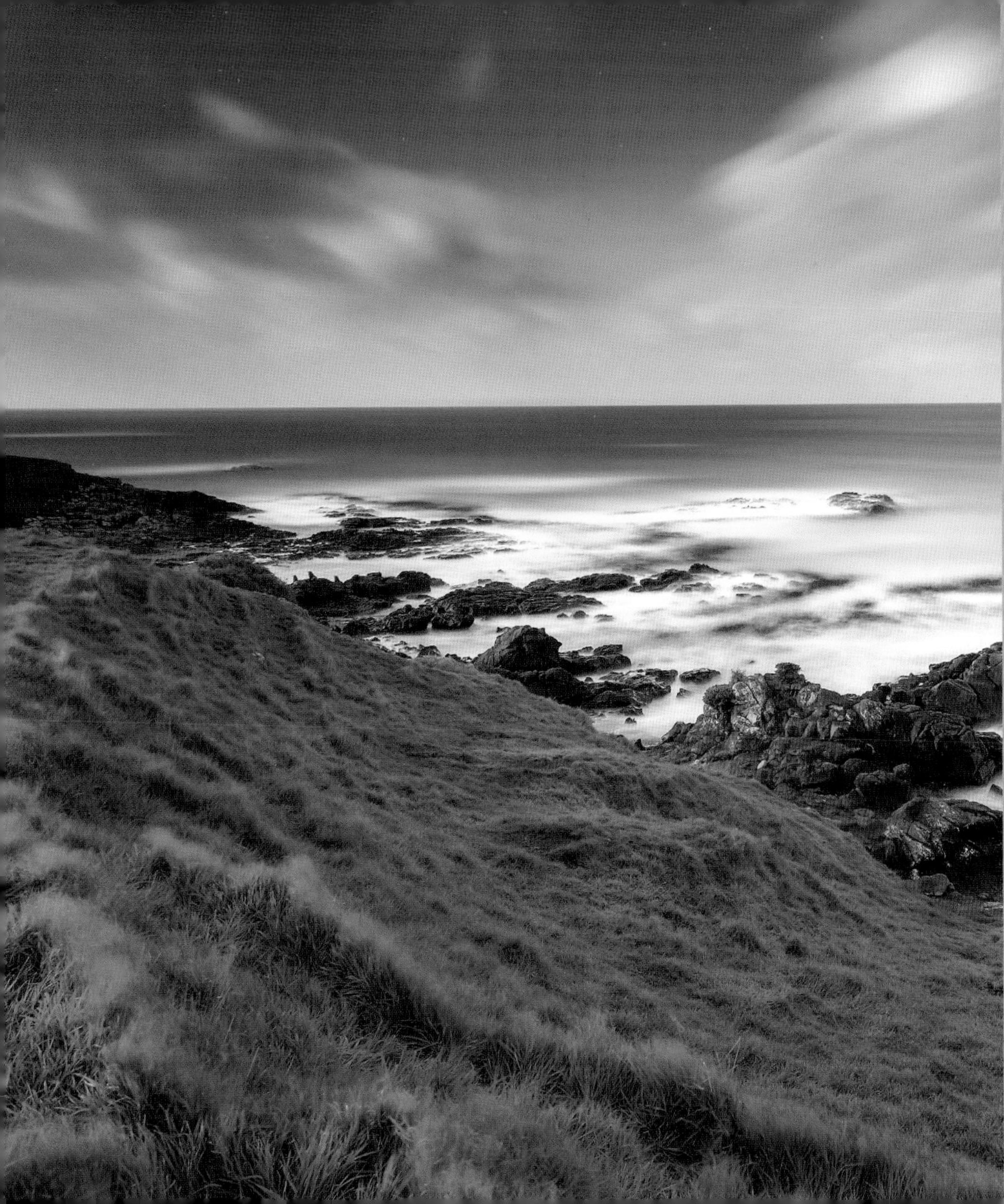

Section 3

Today Is Day One

Robert D. Smith

"Time stays long enough for anyone who will use it."

—Leonardo da Vinci
Italian inventor, architect, painter, scientist, sculptor
b. April 15, 1452, d. May 2, 1519
(He lived exactly 24,488 days)

Robert D. Smith

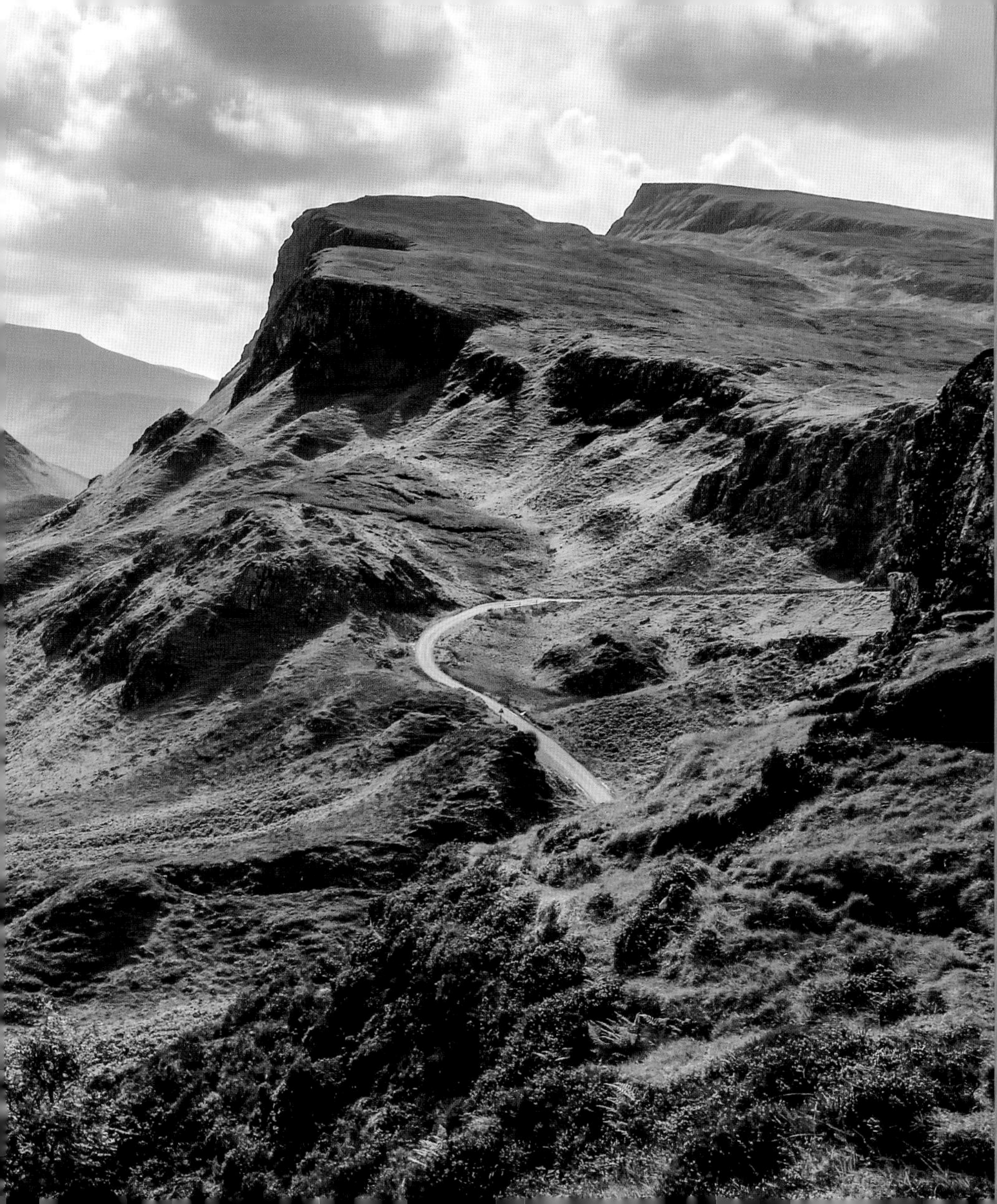

Three Steps to Catapult Your Life

We've made it. Now it's time for the rubber to hit the road. We've talked about mind-set, time, and action. Next, we're going to discuss some practical ways to master your life right now. These are the steps I set out to take as I sat in my hotel suite, recounting the 20,000 days I'd been alive. This is what powered me to act with determination, boldly launching into the future, like a stone from a catapult. These steps gave me the sense of urgency I needed to begin living my next 20,000 days with more intensity and purpose than ever before. I am positive they will do the same for you if you truly push yourself to take them.

Sit down with a notebook or a laptop, and do this for yourself:

Step 1: Determine how many days you have been alive. Are you shocked? Amazed?

Step 2: Determine immediately the answer to these two critical, ongoing questions. (I know you can't be sure about these things, but IF you were, what might they be?)

1. **What is important right now to you?**
2. **What is next for you?**

Having trouble? Here are some thoughts to prompt your answers:

- **What have I not thought of yet?**
- **What is one immediate need I can fill for someone I know?**
- **What is a *huge* dream I have? How can I think bigger?**

Step 3: Draft your life's story, then live it!

That last one sounds like a huge task, I know. But it's easier if you think of it as a biography. I love A&E's TV series *Biography*. Entertainers from all walks of life are featured. Picture your own episode of *Biography* being written. In fact, you can write it now.

This is your show. You are the director, the set designer, and the screenwriter. It is all in your hands. You decide where you start and finish. You guide the day. You create it all. *This* is who you will become.

Here is the CliffsNotes version of my biography in a sentence:

> I am the master of marketing, the magician of management, the emperor of emails, the artist of attachments, and the warrior of WOW!

Your one-sentence biography is for your eyes only. It doesn't have to be something you ever show to others (mine has never been shown to anyone until now), so don't hold anything back. Be fun and creative. Let it speak to your strengths, even if they are abilities that aren't traditionally viewed as strengths. As you can see in my one-sentence biography, I'm someone who is great at writing emails and creating "WOWing" attachments for them…

not exactly traditional strengths, right? But there is tremendous power in owning those "little" things for which you have talent!

So embrace those strengths with pride, write them down, and repeat them to yourself. Follow these steps daily. Continue to ask yourself, "What's important right now? What's next?" You will be shocked at where you end up.

> "*Three o'clock is always too late or too early for anything you want to do.*"

—**Jean-Paul Sartre**
French writer, philosopher
b. June 21, 1905, d. April 15, 1980
(He lived exactly 27,327 days)

Robert D. Smith

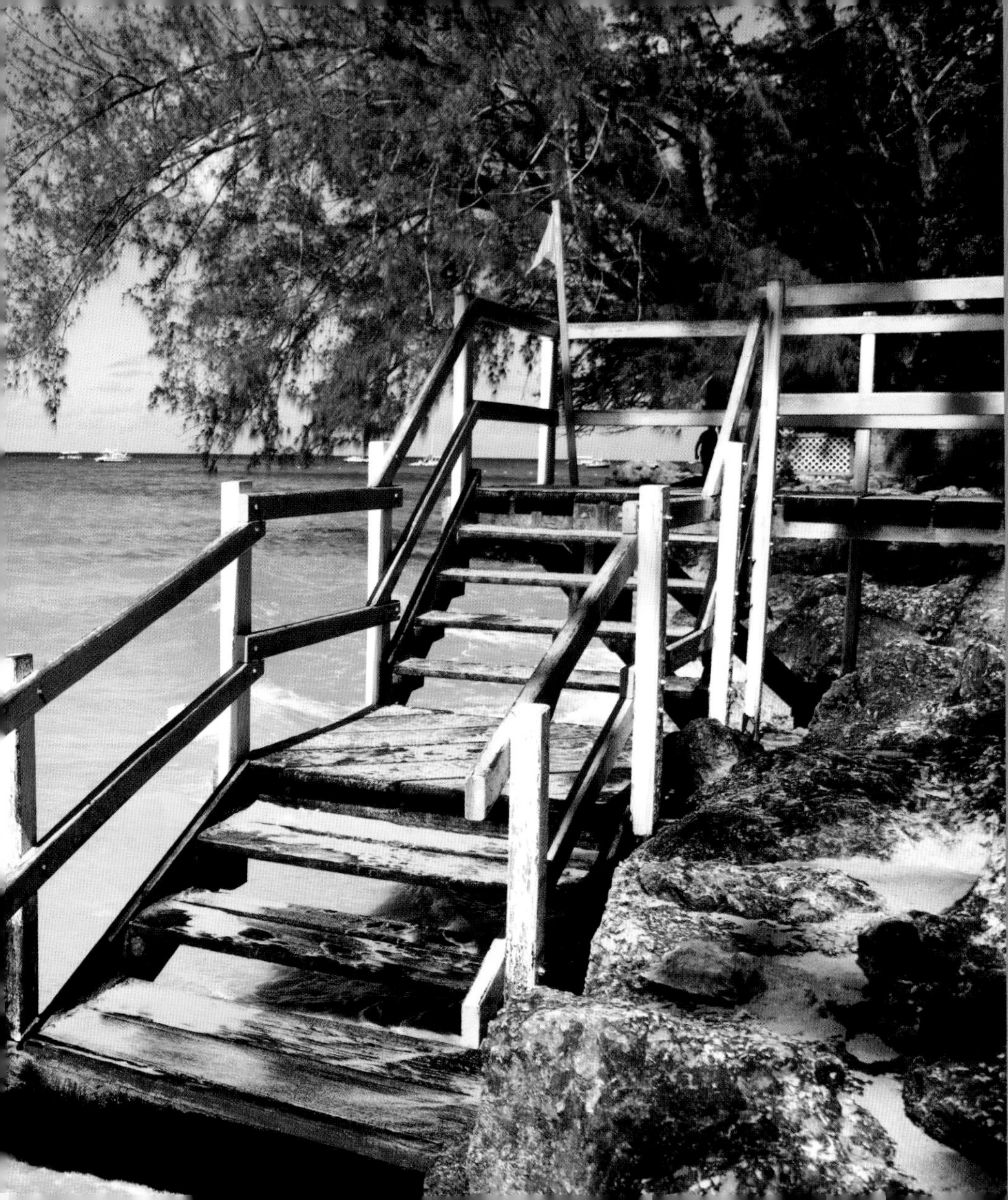

Seven Questions to Seize the Essence of Today

Want to guarantee that you will create intensity every day of your life? Then review these questions, as if for the first time, every single morning you are blessed with another day.

1. Whose life am I going to brighten today?

2. What three things am I most grateful for today?

3. What memories am I going to create today?

4. What challenge am I going to overcome today?

5. What value am I going to create today?

6. How much joy can I create for others and myself today?

7. What life-changing decision(s) am I going to make today?

Robert D. Smith

Bonus question (just to cover all the bases): What question am I not asking yet *today*?

Never be misled by the number of hours in a day. This number simply represents the time that is *potentially available* to you. Each of these moments is but a dab of paint you can apply to the canvas of your life. Somewhere between sunrise and sunset, let it not be said that you lost an hour. No reward can be offered to find lost hours, for they are gone forever. The present moment is the only moment you totally control.

"*Success in the majority of circumstances depends on knowing how long it takes to succeed.*"

—**Charles de Montesquieu**
French jurist, political philosopher
b. January 18, 1689, d. February 10, 1755
(He lived exactly 24,118 days)

Robert D. Smith

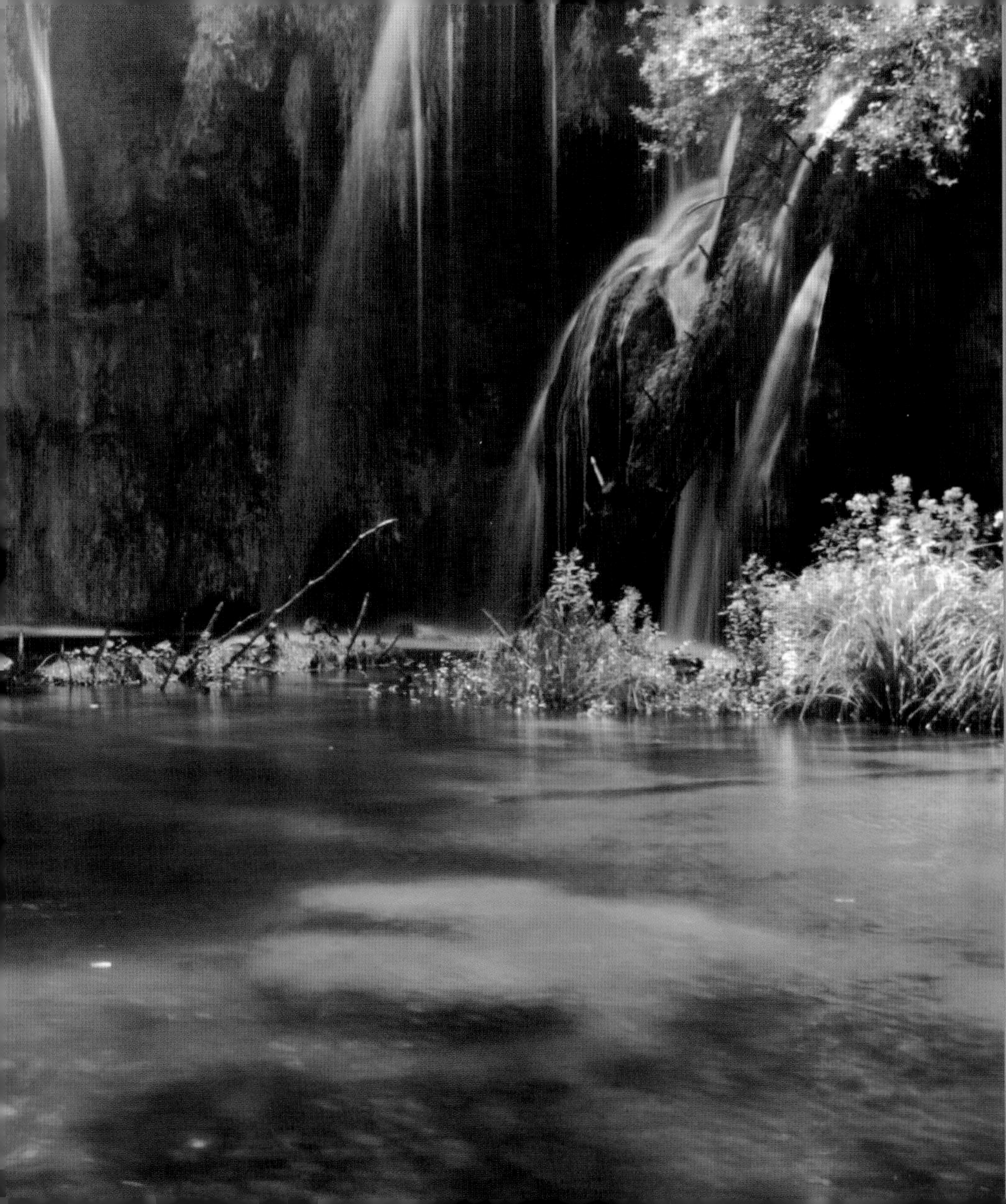

Ten Things You Can Do Now

We have an amazing ability to overestimate what we can do in the next five years and totally underestimate what we can do in the next fifteen minutes.

It seems that we spend 80 percent of our time planning and 20 percent implementing and progressing. Very few can really execute on purpose.

This is not to say that planning is a bad thing. In fact, planning is critical. But a line must be drawn; a distinction must be made. Notice that when I took the time to plan the second 20,000 days of my life, I did it in forty-eight hours. And then I set out to live those days.

Do you know how much time you could spend planning 20,000 days? Some couples take an entire year just to plan their wedding—an event that will be one of the most special memories of their lives, but will last only a few hours.

How much more should you plan for your life's legacy? What

do you most want to be remembered for when you're gone? When would NOW be a good time to make this decision?

Here are ten things you could do in the next fifteen minutes that would make a drastic difference in your day:

1. **Call a family member you have not spoken to in a while. Tell them you love them. Honor them.**

2. **Make a list of the top five priorities in your life today. Prioritize them. Now act on them in order, completing each priority or making major progress on some portion of it.**

3. **Invite a close friend to dinner.**

4. **You know that thing you've been putting off? Do it.**

5. **Begin your next big project, no matter how big it is. When I could not get started on a term paper in high school, my teacher told me, "Starting is half finished." A huge encouragement then—and now.**

6. If you don't have a next big project, come up with one. It can be something as simple as organizing the garage. Or it can be as big as writing a book.

7. Start reading the book you've been meaning to pick up.

8. Exercise. Begin living healthily. Enjoy the gift that is your body.

9. Crank up some of your favorite music and jump around. Dance. Celebrate the day! Celebrate this moment!

10. Go outside and breathe deeply. Be still. Listen. Be grateful. Simply say, thank YOU!

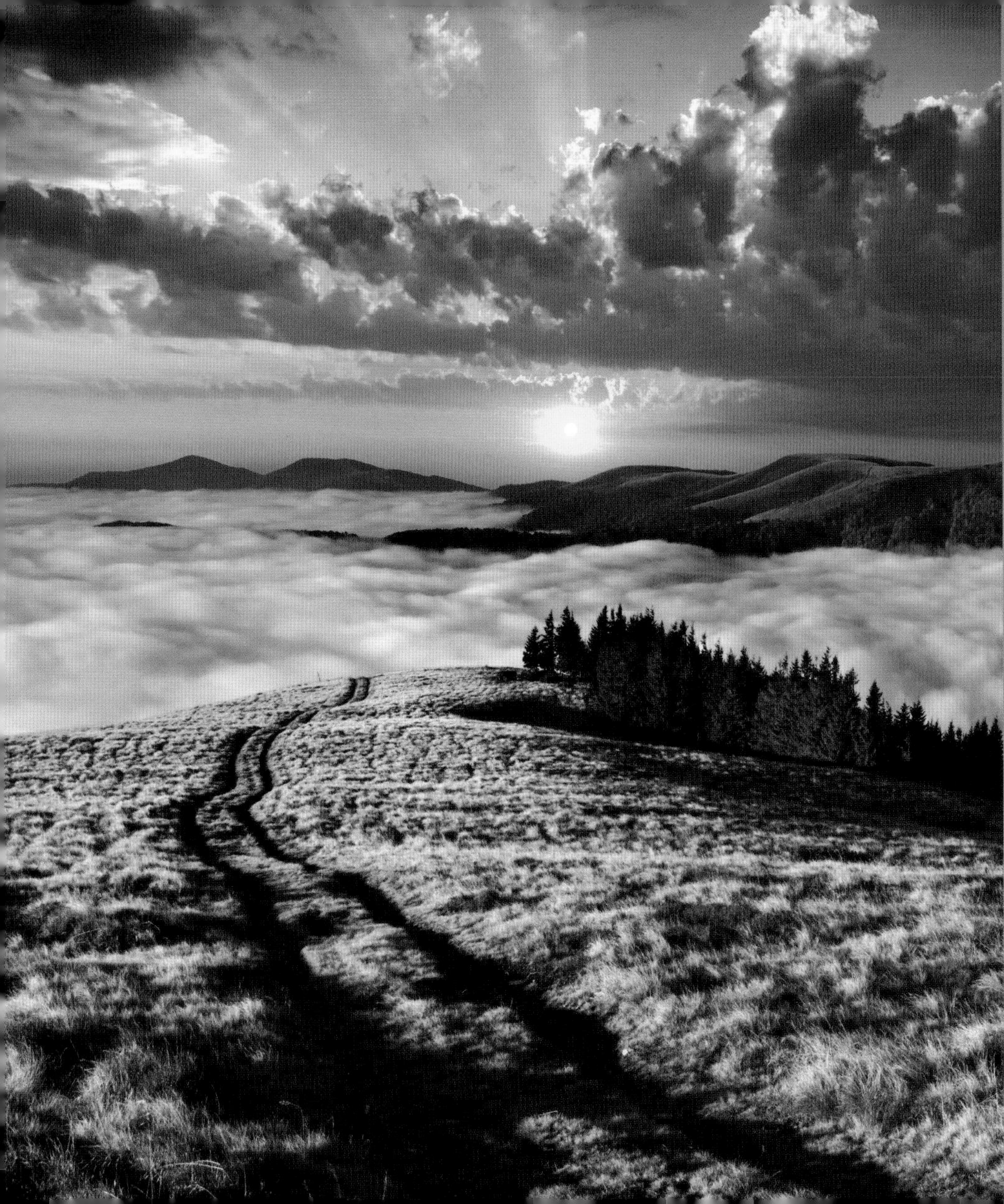

"*In truth, people can generally make time for what they choose to do; it is not really the time but the will that is wanting.*"

—John Lubbock
British statesman, banker, naturalist
b. April 30, 1834, d. May 28, 1913
(He lived exactly 28,882 days)

Robert P. Smith

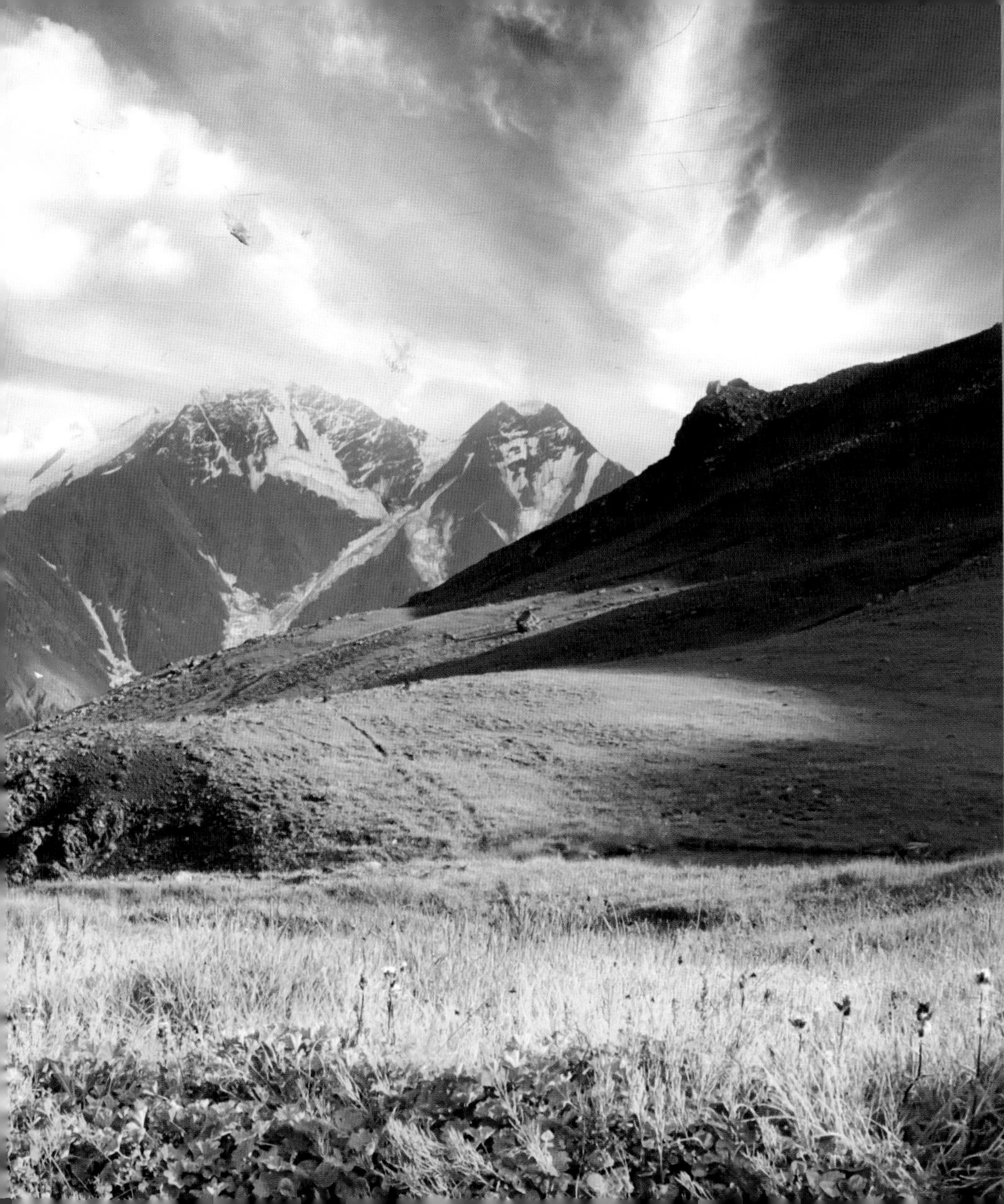

One Final Note:
My Desire for YOU

I wish I could be there in person with you to celebrate who you are becoming, to witness the decisions you are making, and to see you stepping up to a life lived with intensity. But that is the consequence of the distance between us. So I'm writing you this note and sending all my best wishes with it. I'm very proud of you! Keep reaching into your bold, new future. Keep counting *up* your days. Cherish every second, every minute, every moment. Seize them all—to accomplish, to celebrate, to act.

Be your best self and do not imitate anyone else. Find *your* strengths. They are your talents. They will make you smile and cause you to experience real joy on the inside.

Don't listen to those who ridicule the choices you make or the dreams you share. Let no one despise your youth. As Og Mandino

Robert D. Smith

explained in *The Greatest Salesman in the World*, "Experience is overrated, usually by old men who nod wisely and speak stupidly." Create your own experiences. And know that you are creating memories for a lifetime.

Life is not about finding yourself; it is about creating yourself.

You have to take chances to make your dreams reality. Face your fear head-on and move rapidly. Don't be afraid of making mistakes. Make lots of them! Your odds for success will increase with the number of decisions you make.

Have patience with your dreams and the expectations you have for others. Be impatient with yourself daily. Live as if this is your last day. Say "I love you" to all those who matter. Know that everyone matters.

You must play full-out right now. Sit up. Hold your head high. Breathe deeply. Lift your chest up. Stand straight and with confidence. Dust yourself off. Stop being a party pooper in your own life. Smile. A bigger, noticeable smile. Start acting happy. Yes, you act first. I promise the feeling of happiness will soon follow.

When I left that hotel room forty-eight hours later, I had a sense of purpose and direction like never before in my life. Do you know what it feels like to wake up every day with the absolute certainty that what you will be doing every hour of that day will add up to something much larger than you? If you don't know what that feels like, I promise you can. There's no secret trick or complicated formula you have to follow. All it takes is for you simply to decide that you are going to live your life with purpose, and that you will never stop chasing that purpose as long as you're still breathing.

Decisions you make right now can change your life forever. Literally forever. You do not choose to be born. You do not choose your parents. You do not choose the time period in which you live. You do not choose the country of your birth. You do not choose the circumstances of your upbringing. In most cases, you do not choose to die. You do not choose the time or conditions of your death.

Despite all the realms of this choicelessness, *we do choose how we will live.* May you have a glorious ending by beginning today.

One Final Life Quote

Robert D. Smith

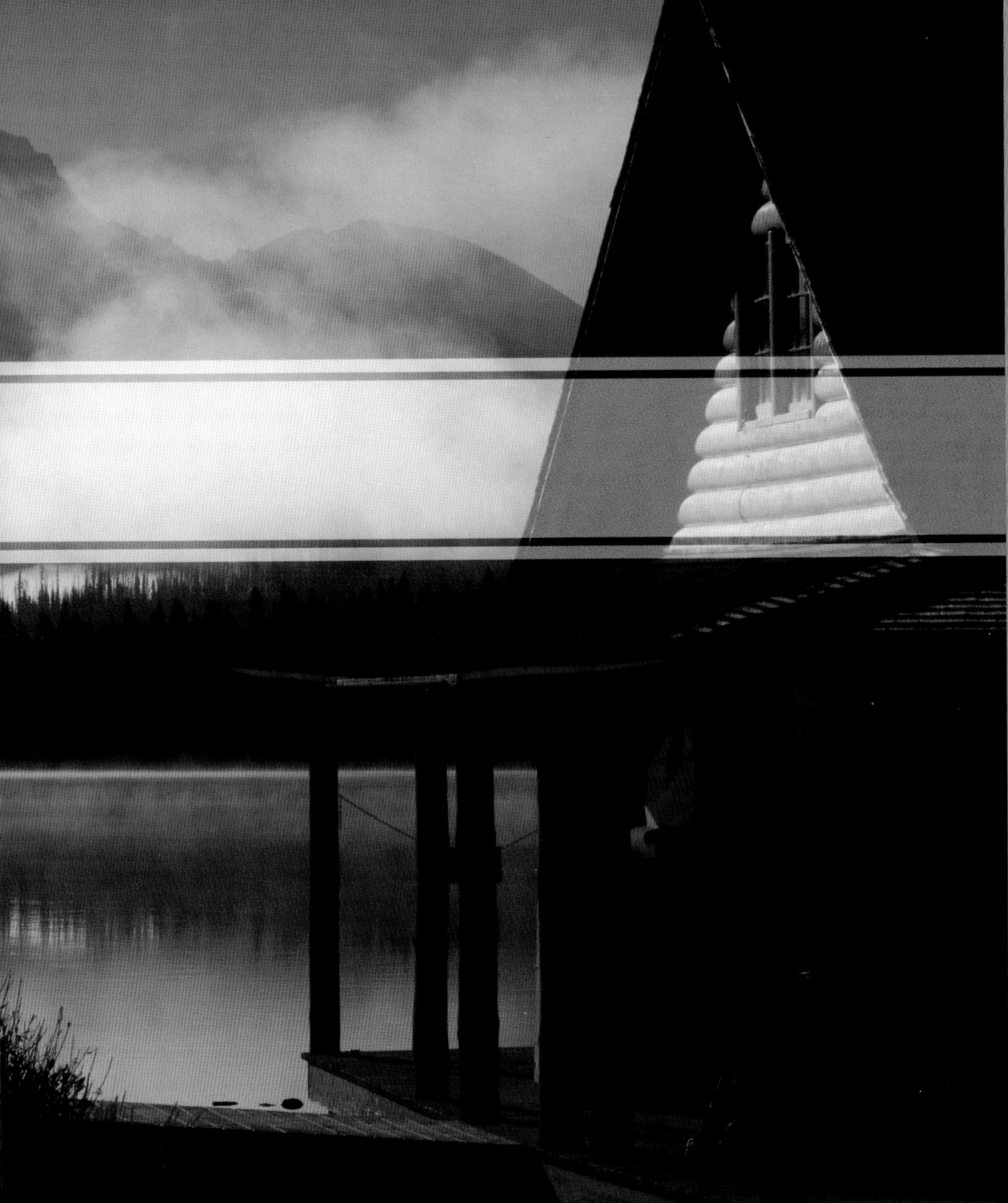

20,000 Days...and Counting

"We all run on two clocks. One is the outside clock, which ticks away our decades and brings us ceaselessly to the dry season. The other is the inside clock, where you are your own timekeeper and determine your own chronology, your own internal

Robert D. Smith

weather, and your own rate of living. Sometimes the inner clock runs itself out long before the outer one, and you see a dead man going through the motions of living."

—**Max Lerner**
American author, columnist
b. December 20, 1902, d. June 5, 1992
(He lived exactly 32,675 days)

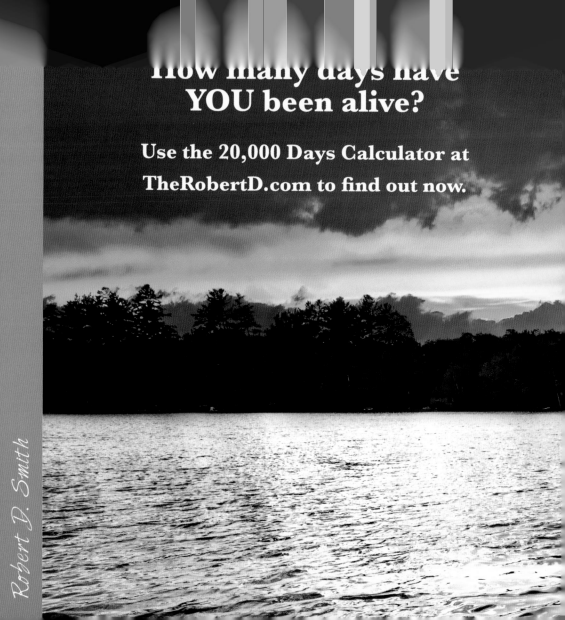

How many days have
YOU been alive?

Use the 20,000 Days Calculator at
TheRobertD.com to find out now.

Robert D. Smith

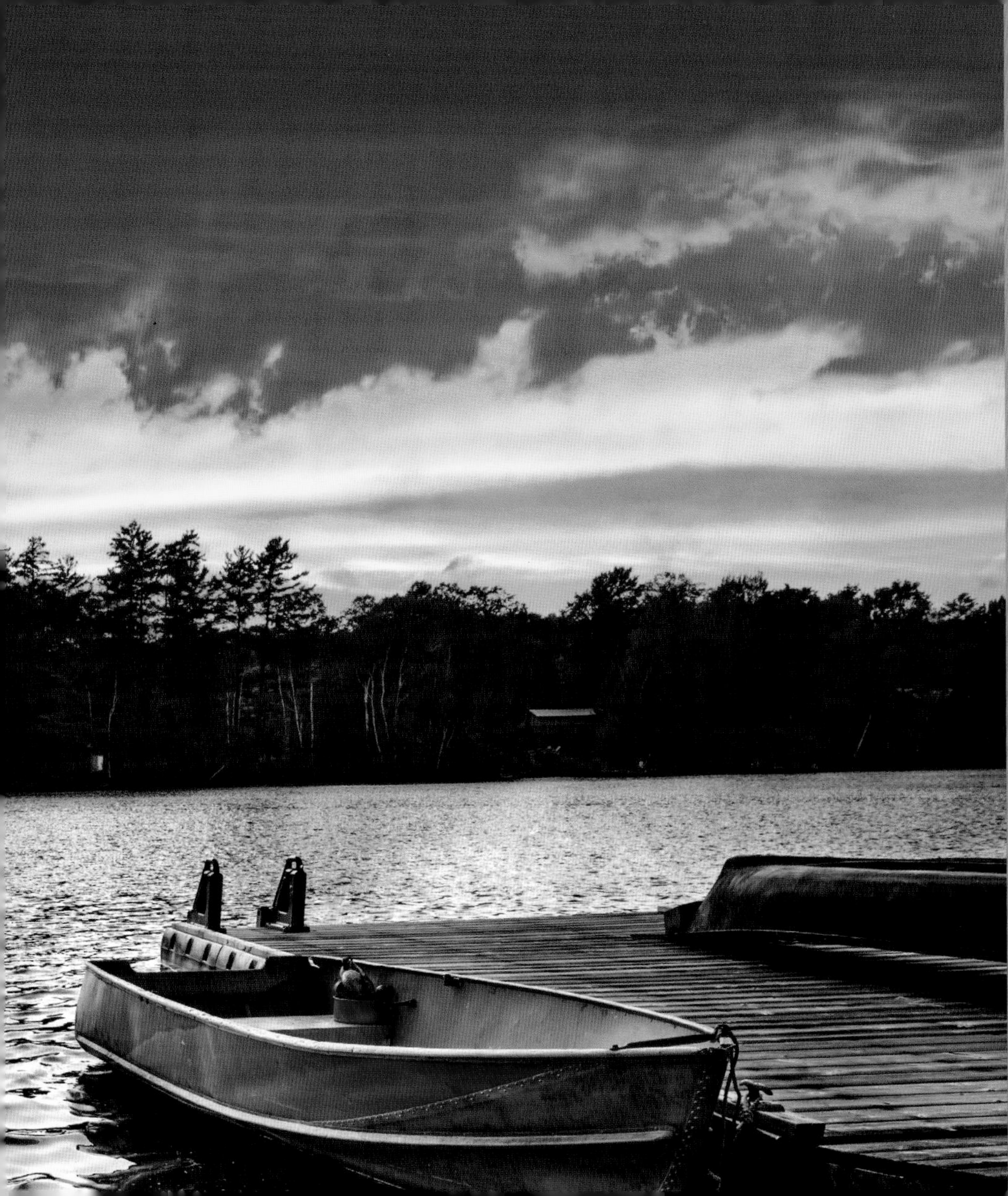

Acknowledgments

No book is published solely because of the author. It takes more time, effort, and energy from others than most would imagine. Thank you all for your presence in my life and the things you did to help make this possible.

Family is critical. Mom and Dad are imperative. They are the ingredients that were combined in the first two decades of my life that allowed me to be me. They laid the foundation of who I became. Thank you all—Mom (Juanita), Dad (Robert Lee), and my three wonderful sisters (Lisa Evans, Sandy Martin, and Marlisa Smith).

To Andy Andrews: When we started out together over thirty years ago, I told you I would be your manager until you found someone else. I hope you've stopped looking.

To Polly, Austin, and Adam Andrews: I'm *sooo* honored to be a part of your family.

To Scott Jeffrey, a friend for life, whose guidance touched this book in more ways than one.

To Stephanie DeMizio, whose insight was invaluable to this book's development.

To Mac Anderson: It is a joy to do business with you as a publisher, but it is an honor to call you a friend. And to the dozens of wonderful people at Sourcebooks who had a hand in releasing this book, including Lynn Harker and Brian Frantz (who made this book look so great); Alice Patenaude (thank you for your editorial assistance!); and Heather Hall (thanks for overseeing production on this book).

All of you have affected my life in ways I never could have predicted. Here's to our next 20,000 days together!

About the Author

Credit: Engracia Hombrados

For more than three decades, Robert D. Smith has spent his career in the place he loves most—behind the scenes and away from the spotlight. He has overseen from its inception the career of Andy Andrews, a *New York Times* bestselling author and in-demand speaker.

He has served as a private consultant to numerous bestselling authors, speakers, entertainers, and organizations, educating them on the methods he has employed to sustain massive success across multiple industries for the past thirty-plus years.

His unique lifestyle, magnetic personality, and uncanny ability to get the best out of those with whom he works make him the ideal person to convey the proven strategies described in *20,000 Days... and Counting* to an eager and waiting audience.

Don't miss two life-changing books by Andy Andrews:

The Perfect Moment and *The Butterfly Effect*.

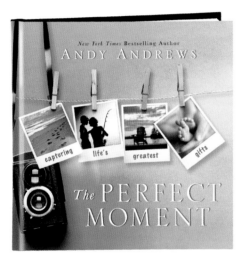

The Butterfly Effect is an unforgettable story about how our world is filled with incredible lives of permanent purpose.

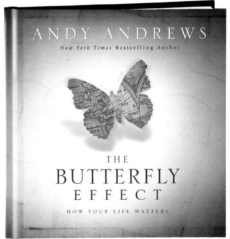

The Perfect Moment will change the way you look at life forever.

For more information, visit TheRobertD.com.